MACAT

An Analysis of

Jack A. Goldstone's

Revolution and Rebellion in the Early Modern World

Etienne Stockland

Published by Macat International Ltd
24:13 Coda Centre, 189 Munster Road, London SW6 6AW.

Distributed exclusively by Routledge
2 Park Square, Milton Park, Abingdon, Oxon OX14 4RN
711 Third Avenue, New York, NY 10017, USA

Routledge is an imprint of the Taylor & Francis Group, an informa business

www.macat.com
info@macat.com

Cataloguing in Publication Data
A catalogue record for this book is available from the British Library.
Library of Congress Cataloguing-in-Publication Data is available upon request.
Cover illustration: A. Richard Allen

ISBN 978-1-912303-77-9 (hardback)
ISBN 978-1-912128-50-1 (paperback)
ISBN 978-1-912282-65-4 (e-book)

Notice

CONTENTS

THE MACAT LIBRARY

The Macat Library is a series of unique academic explorations of seminal works in the humanities and social sciences – books and papers that have had a significant and widely recognised impact on their disciplines. It has been created to serve as much more than just a summary of what lies between the covers of a great book. It illuminates and explores the influences on, ideas of, and impact of that book. Our goal is to offer a learning resource that encourages critical thinking and fosters a better, deeper understanding of important ideas.

Each publication is divided into three Sections: Influences, Ideas, and Impact. Each Section has four Modules. These explore every important facet of the work, and the responses to it.

This Section-Module structure makes a Macat Library book easy to use, but it has another important feature. Because each Macat book is written to the same format, it is possible (and encouraged!) to cross-reference multiple Macat books along the same lines of inquiry or research. This allows the reader to open up interesting interdisciplinary pathways.

To further aid your reading, lists of glossary terms and people mentioned are included at the end of this book (these are indicated by an asterisk [*] throughout) – as well as a list of works cited.

Macat has worked with the University of Cambridge to identify the elements of critical thinking and understand the ways in which six different skills combine to enable effective thinking.
Three allow us to fully understand a problem; three more give us the tools to solve it. Together, these six skills make up the **PACIER** model of critical thinking. They are:

ANALYSIS – understanding how an argument is built
EVALUATION – exploring the strengths and weaknesses of an argument
INTERPRETATION – understanding issues of meaning

CREATIVE THINKING – coming up with new ideas and fresh connections
PROBLEM-SOLVING – producing strong solutions
REASONING – creating strong arguments

To find out more, visit **WWW.MACAT.COM.**

CRITICAL THINKING AND *REVOLUTION AND REBELLION IN THE EARLY MODERN WORLD*

Primary critical thinking skill: PROBLEM-SOLVING
Secondary critical thinking skill: EVALUATION

Understanding why revolutions take place when they do, and as they do, is important in itself. Understanding how they are rooted in the societies they upend – and the ways in which those societies share crucial similarities – is arguably even more so.

The enduring influence of Jack Goldstone's *Revolution and Rebellion* lies as much in the challenge that it issues to the long-dominant model of 'western exceptionalism' (the idea that it was early modern Europe's distinctive history that launched it on the path to world domination) as it does in the book's persuasive account of revolutions rooted in a four stage process that advances from fiscal crisis, through inter-elite conflict and mass-mobilization potential, to the breakdown and re-making of culture and ideology.

It can be argued that this unexpected outcome – one that the author himself did not anticipate – is the product of an acute problem-solving ability, one that made Goldstone particularly receptive to alternative possibilities. His insistence that early modern and modern European and Asian peoples have vastly more in common than was generally recognised, and followed a similar path of advanced organic development that left Qing China as vulnerable to revolution as the France of the Ancien Régime, has not only become a central contention of early 21st century sociology; it has also underpinned the creation of multiple theoretical models that have nothing to do with revolution. None of this would have been possible had not Goldstone challenged himself by asking questions that other scholars had supposed had mundane answers.

ABOUT THE AUTHOR OF THE ORIGINAL WORK

American sociologist and political scientist **Jack A. Goldstone** was born in 1953, the son of German Jewish immigrants who lived in China during World War II. He earned his doctorate from Harvard before embarking on an academic career, while also providing the American intelligence community with reports on the political stability of regions of strategic interest. In 1993 Goldstone was awarded the American Sociological Association Distinguished Scholarly Book Award for his 1991 work *Revolution and Rebellion in the Early Modern World*. This is one of the highest honors awarded in the field of sociology. Goldstone has since occupied a number of important public policy advisory positions within the United States government, and his thinking has been important to the US intelligence community's forecasting of terrorism trends.

ABOUT THE AUTHOR OF THE ANALYSIS

Etienne Stockland is researching a PhD in environmental history at Columbia University.

ABOUT MACAT

GREAT WORKS FOR CRITICAL THINKING

Macat is focused on making the ideas of the world's great thinkers accessible and comprehensible to everybody, everywhere, in ways that promote the development of enhanced critical thinking skills.

It works with leading academics from the world's top universities to produce new analyses that focus on the ideas and the impact of the most influential works ever written across a wide variety of academic disciplines. Each of the works that sit at the heart of its growing library is an enduring example of great thinking. But by setting them in context – and looking at the influences that shaped their authors, as well as the responses they provoked – Macat encourages readers to look at these classics and game-changers with fresh eyes. Readers learn to think, engage and challenge their ideas, rather than simply accepting them.

'Macat offers an amazing first-of-its-kind tool for interdisciplinary learning and research. Its focus on works that transformed their disciplines and its rigorous approach, drawing on the world's leading experts and educational institutions, opens up a world-class education to anyone.'

Andreas Schleicher
Director for Education and Skills, Organisation for Economic Co-operation and Development

'Macat is taking on some of the major challenges in university education ... They have drawn together a strong team of active academics who are producing teaching materials that are novel in the breadth of their approach.'

Prof Lord Broers,
former Vice-Chancellor of the University of Cambridge

'The Macat vision is exceptionally exciting. It focuses upon new modes of learning which analyse and explain seminal texts which have profoundly influenced world thinking and so social and economic development. It promotes the kind of critical thinking which is essential for any society and economy.
This is the learning of the future.'

Rt Hon Charles Clarke, former UK Secretary of State for Education

'The Macat analyses provide immediate access to the critical conversation surrounding the books that have shaped their respective discipline, which will make them an invaluable resource to all of those, students and teachers, working in the field.'

Professor William Tronzo, University of California at San Diego

WAYS IN TO THE TEXT

KEY POINTS

- Jack A. Goldstone (b. 1953) is an American sociologist* (a scholar of the nature and history of human societies) who specializes in the sociology of revolutions—the overthrow of political or social systems.

- *Revolution and Rebellion* (1991) argued that demographic* factors (that is, matters related to the makeup of a population) caused the revolutions and rebellions that swept across Eurasia* (the continents of Europe and Asia) in the early modern* period (roughly, the late fifteenth to the late eighteenth centuries).

- *Revolution and Rebellion* provides a unique, wide-ranging account of the global rebellions that swept across Eurasia in the seventeenth and eighteenth centuries.

Who Is Jack Goldstone?

Jack A. Goldstone (b. 1953), the author of *Revolution and Rebellion in the Early Modern World* (1991), is an eminent sociologist whose work has focused on political instability and revolutions in Eurasia. Goldstone completed his PhD at Harvard University in 1981 under the supervision of the sociologist Theda Skocpol.* While serving as a sociologist at Northwestern University, the California Institute of Technology, and the University of California at Davis, he also worked for the American intelligence community. As part of a consultation with the United States government in 1984, he evaluated the risk of revolution in the Philippines and successfully predicted the fall of the dictator Ferdinand Marcos's* regime.

Since the publication of *Revolution and Rebellion* in 1991, Goldstone has occupied a number of important public policy advisory positions with the United States government. In the 1990s, he joined the Political Instability Task Force, a group funded by the Central Intelligence Agency (CIA),* which uses statistical modeling to predict state failures in regions of interest to the United States.

In the same decade he became part of the Environmental Change and Security Program, a group funded by the United States Agency for International Development that investigates how population dynamics affect issues of national and international security.[1] As part of both organizations, Goldstone advanced his thesis as to how the crucial variable of demographics indicates the stability and security of states— turning his attention from the early modern Eurasian world to the failed states of modern Africa and Central Asia.

What Does *Revolution and Rebellion* Say?

In *Revolution and Rebellion*, Goldstone develops a universal model for explaining the causes of revolutions in the early modern world that consists of four variables:

- "Fiscal crisis": periods of acute financial stress that result from rapid population growth. Goldstone shows how demographic changes in states produce rapid inflation* and increasing demands on resources, conditions further complicated by remarkably inflexible taxation systems.
- "Intra-elite conflict":* conflict and competition between social and economic elites that stem from population change. When states fail to absorb more elites into the system of patronage, and provide them with positions in the state administration,

resentment and frustration follow, resulting in a disgruntled population that believes it will profit from overthrowing the existing regime.

- "Mass-mobilization potential"* of the popular classes: Goldstone argues that when economic growth cannot keep pace with a growing population, this leads to widespread poverty, unemployment, and vagrancy. Disgruntled elites seize on these popular grievances when seeking to overthrow existing political institutions.
- "Culture and ideology"—a critical factor for shaping institutions in the period that follows the breakdown of a state. In this final phase of the revolutionary process, new institutions are erected based on ideologies that address the grievances of both elites and popular classes marginalized under the old regime.

These four variables both provide the structure for *Revolution and Rebellion* and constitute the model used to explain Goldstone's theory of revolutions. In successive chapters, Goldstone tests his theory through a comparative analysis of the English Revolution* of 1642–51 (a conflict between supporters of the English Parliament and forces loyal to the English monarch* Charles I); the French Revolution* of 1789–99 (a period that saw the overthrow of the monarchy, and the establishment of a republican government); the Ottoman Crises* of the first decades of the twentieth century, which saw the collapse of the Turkish empire in 1922; the fall of the Chinese Ming* and Qing* dynasties (1644 and 1911 respectively); and the collapse of the Japanese Tokugawa* military dynasty in 1868.

Showing how these states each faced the first three variables (demographically induced fiscal crises, intra-elite conflict and mass-mobilization potential), he offers a panoramic view of the stress fractures that ran through the states of early modern Eurasia—and that ultimately led to their collapse.

A final section on state reconstruction provides the key to understanding the divergent paths taken by Eastern and Western states. Different cultural frameworks governed reactions to state breakdown and the reconstruction phase. Persistence of a "tradition-repudiating" ideology* (a set of political beliefs that, in this case, argued for the overturn of traditional practices) in France and England, and of tradition-enforcing ideologies in the Middle East and East Asia, had long-lasting influence on the shape of these social and political systems following their collapse.

Why Does *Revolution and Rebellion* Matter?

The argument that Eurasia was structurally similar over the long term (from 1500–1800) has proved to be one of the book's most influential claims—even more than Goldstone's demographic/structural model of revolutions. At the time that *Revolution and Rebellion* was published, this claim for a fundamental structural unity shared by Europe and Asia was secondary. Yet the book has unexpectedly become an important text in the discipline of sociology.

Goldstone's *Revolution and Rebellion* challenged conventional accounts of Western modernization* (the process through which a society passes from a "traditional" to a "modern" society) and provoked an ongoing intellectual debate about both the nature and periodization* (how historical periods are divided) of Western modernity. Sociologists traditionally followed the German economist and political philosopher Karl Marx* and the pioneering German sociologist Max Weber* in assuming that early modern Europe's distinctive history allowed it to develop dynamic economic and political institutions that launched it on the path to global supremacy. In particular, the transition from feudalism* (an economic and social system based on the holding of agricultural land in exchange for rents, labor, and services) to capitalism* (an economic and social system in which trade and industry are held in private hands), which began in the sixteenth century, produced long-term structural transformations that ushered in rapid economic and political modernization.

But Goldstone challenged this interpretation with his theory of Eurasian similarity; he argued that from 1500 to 1800, "the major states of Europe, China, India and the Ottoman Empire were all experiencing a similar course of advanced organic development."[2] The thesis found a number of followers in the 1990s—scholars who came to be known collectively as the "California School"*—and it has recently become a central contention in sociology, because it challenges the long-standing assumption that Western Europe had achieved a higher degree of economic development than Asia before the Industrial Revolution* of the eighteenth century (the period of technological innovation and transformation of industrial production between about 1760 and 1840).

Because Goldstone has since provided a more sophisticated and elaborate defense of this thesis, works that he has written subsequent to *Revolution and Rebellion* have proved to be the main rallying point for proponents and opponents.[3] But if the California School thesis can be traced back to *Revolution and Rebellion*, this work arguably gave birth to an influential movement in the disciplines of history and sociology—meaning that it launched a revolution in its own right.

NOTES

1 An early report from this group emphasized the importance of demographic factors as a cause of state failures in Africa and Central Asia. Jack A. Goldstone et al., "The State Failure Project: Early Warning Research for US Foreign Policy Planning," in *Preventive Measures: Building Risk Assessments and Crisis Early Warning Systems*, ed. John L. Davies and T.R. Gurr (Boulder, CO: Rowman and Littlefield, 1998), 27–38.

2 Jack A. Goldstone, "Capitalist Origins, the Advent of Modernity, and Coherent Explanation: A Response to Joseph M. Bryant," *Canadian Journal of Sociology* 33 (Winter 2008): 120.

3   See for example Jack A. Goldstone, "Gender, Work, and Culture: Why the Industrial Revolution came Early to England and Late to China," *Sociological Perspectives* 39 (1996): 1–21; "The Problem of the 'Early Modern' World," *Journal of the Economic and Social History of the Orient* 41, no. 3 (1998): 249–84; "The Rise of the West – or Not? A Revision to Socio-Economic History," *Sociological Theory* 18 (2000): 157–94; *Why Europe? The Rise of the West in World History 1500-1850* (New York: McGraw-Hill, 2008).

SECTION 1
INFLUENCES

MODULE 1
THE AUTHOR AND THE HISTORICAL CONTEXT

KEY POINTS

- With *Revolution and Rebellion*, Goldstone made a crucial contribution to the field of conflict theory* (inquiry into how material, political, and social inequalities produce conflicts between different social groups).

- While completing his doctoral dissertation at Harvard, Goldstone worked with Theda Skocpol,* a historical sociologist* who had a profound influence on his work.

- Goldstone's *Revolution and Rebellion* was partly an attempt to understand the wave of revolutions and state failures that swept the globe from the late 1970s to the early 1990s.

Why Read This Text?

A seminal work of sociology (the study of the functioning and nature of human societies) and comparative history* (which compares the characteristics of different societies within the same historical period), Jack A. Goldstone's *Revolution and Rebellion in the Early Modern World* (1991) seeks to explain the causes of state breakdown in Europe and Asia from the seventeenth to nineteenth centuries.

Goldstone builds his analysis on the premise that the states of early modern Eurasia were "not greatly different from each other."[1] Their economies were "overwhelmingly agrarian"* (based on agriculture) and politically managed by large bureaucracies directed by hereditary rulers.[2] He argues that states in Britain, France, the Near East, China, and Japan faced similar pressures that led to outbreaks of violence and political opposition.

❝ Most political scientists and historians have underestimated the role of demography in political crises by thinking only about aggregate population changes. They have thereby overlooked the disproportionate impact that even moderate overall population change has on particular groups—urban workers, landless peasants, the young, and noninheriting offspring of elites—as well as the massive indirect effects of population change on prices, government revenues, and income distribution. ❞

Jack A. Goldstone, *Revolution and Rebellion in the Early Modern World*

Revolution and Rebellion is a crucial contribution to conflict theory, a field of sociology that traces its origins back to the works of two Germans, the political philosopher Karl Marx* and the sociologist Max Weber.* Conflict theorists ask: what makes social groups mobilize against dominant political elites, and under what conditions do challenges to central authority become successful? Explaining the causes of social conflict and political revolutions is fundamental to the discipline of sociology. In answering a relatively long-standing problem in the field, Goldstone developed a novel theory of revolutions—one that emphasized how long-term demographic* factors (factors associated with the makeup of populations) could destabilize centralized states* (roughly, states in which a system of central government operates).

Author's Life
Goldstone was born in 1953, the son of German Jewish immigrants who lived in China during World War II.* As a doctoral student at Harvard University, Goldstone studied under three eminent social theorists:* Shmuel N. Eisenstadt,* George Homans,* and Theda

Skocpol. These scholars sparked his interest in long-term social transformations, political revolutions, and comparative history.

Goldstone's mentor, Theda Skocpol, left a profound theoretical and methodological imprint on his thought; his concept of state breakdown is indebted to her. Skocpol's seminal book *States and Social Revolutions* (1979) identified the debilitating weaknesses of central states as the primary cause of revolutionary conflicts.[3] Moreover, like Goldstone, Skocpol developed her theory of revolution through a comparative study of Asian and Western experiences of social and political revolutions.

Revolution and Rebellion was published in 1991, while Goldstone was serving as professor of sociology and international relations at the University of California at Davis. At that time, he was also the founding director of the Center for Comparative Research in History, Society and Culture (later renamed the Center for History, Society, and Culture). Through this institution, Goldstone helped to promote macro-comparative* historical sociology. He learned this scholarly approach—which attempts to discern the general structural patterns that lead to revolutions, for example—from his mentor.

Author's Background

Goldstone's interest in social conflict and political revolution theories stemmed from the sociopolitical environment in which he studied and worked. The core ideas developed in *Revolution and Rebellion* spoke in a very direct way to the preoccupations of the period. A wave of revolutions and state failures swept across the world between the 1970s and 1990s, toppling regimes in Iran (the Iranian Revolution* of 1979 replaced a monarchical* dynasty with an Islamic regime), Nicaragua*, the Philippines (the Yellow Revolution* of 1983 to 1986 overturned the dictatorship of Ferdinand Marcos* in favor of democratic government), Afghanistan (in the Saur Revolution* of 1978, the communist* People's Democratic Party overthrew the sitting president)—and perhaps most dramatically in the Soviet Union,* which saw its satellite states break into separate nations and the arrival of democracy in Russia in 1991.

These revolutions and state breakdowns caught many policymakers and academics by surprise, and led Goldstone's contemporaries to search for their causes. This wave also stimulated historical and sociological research into the nature of revolutions. The unstable global political climate of the 1970s and 1980s virtually demanded such research, as policymakers needed knowledge that would enable them to predict and address future conflicts and revolutions. And so Goldstone and his contemporaries used historical comparative sociology* to understand global instability and social conflict. Not only was their work timely from an academic standpoint; it was the response to a global imperative.

NOTES

1   Jack A. Goldstone, *Revolution and Rebellion in the Early Modern World* (Berkeley: University of California Press, 1991), 4.

2   Goldstone, *Revolution and Rebellion*, 4.

3   Theda Skocpol, *States and Social Revolutions: A Comparative Analysis of France, Russia and China* (Cambridge: Cambridge University Press, 1979).

MODULE 2
ACADEMIC CONTEXT

KEY POINTS

- The field of "conflict theory"* in the discipline of sociology*
  seeks to understand what causes social conflict and
  political revolutions.

- The comparative sociology of revolutions*—an approach
  used by social scientists to compare the characteristics of
  different societies that have experienced revolutions—was
  an approach that grew in popularity from the 1960s onward.

- Goldstone placed the study of demographic* trends (trends
  in the makeup of nations' populations) at the center of the
  sociology of revolutions.

The Work in its Context

Jack A. Goldstone's *Revolution and Rebellion in the Early Modern World*
contributes to the field of "conflict theory," a branch of sociology that
seeks to explain what causes social conflict and political revolutions. In
the United States, this tradition became dominant in the 1960s, as the
collapse of McCarthyism* (a period of heightened fear of
communism* in the United States between 1950 and 1954) allowed
ideas inspired by the work of the political philosopher Karl Marx* to
flourish in American universities. At the same time, a school of
thinkers—notably the American sociologists Barrington Moore Jr.,*
Charles Tilly,* and Theda Skocpol*—began to use the methods of
comparative history* to develop theories of revolution.[1] These
scholars compared revolutions across different historical and
geographical contexts, with the goal of pinpointing their
transhistorical* and transcultural* causes (the historical and cultural

> ❝ Given the explosive population growth that has occurred in the Third World during the twentieth century, often without the benefit of rapid industrialization or flexible political institutions, it is not surprising that this is a 'century of revolution' in Third World states. ❞
>
> Jack Goldstone, *Revolution and Rebellion in the Early Modern World*

features common to nations that have experienced revolution).

But *Revolution and Rebellion* differed from the pioneering works of conflict theory in one important respect: it identified long-term demographic factors as the prime cause of social conflict and political revolutions. For Goldstone, political revolutions occur when population growth outstrips the level of economic development. This leads to fiscal crises,* disaffected elites who no longer support the state, and popular unrest. Rapid population increases destabilize absolutist agrarian states* (states ruled by a single leader, which derive the majority of their revenues from agricultural production) by stretching their limited fiscal capabilities; this renders them unable to provide for their subjects. So, in short, revolutions occur when rapid population increases weaken states' economic and political power—and challenge their ability to control subordinate groups as a result.

Overview of the Field

Goldstone's *Revolution and Rebellion* holds an important place in historical demography,* a field many sociologists neglected at the time of the book's publication. His attempt to explain revolutions through long-term population trends proved highly innovative and controversial, especially since he drew inspiration from the works of the English economist Thomas Malthus* at a time when Malthusianism* (an approach to social analysis that investigates the relationship between social stability and population trends) had fallen out of favor among social scientists.

Goldstone was also one of the first sociologists to embrace the work of two pioneering demographic historians: Peter Laslett* and Edward Anthony Wrigley,* who founded the Cambridge Group for the History of Population and Social Structure in 1964. As Goldstone remarked in *Revolution and Rebellion*, "The notion that population change was at the root of large-scale historical change has often been considered, and just as often been quickly dismissed."[2]

At the same time, political scientists had increasingly started to pay attention to how rapid population growth affected the stability of centralized states,* particularly in the developing world. The postwar period's "population bomb"—a term coined by the biologist Paul. R. Ehrlich* to describe the unsustainability of population growth—was increasingly seen as a source of social and political instability. Goldstone himself stressed that his demographic account of state failures in early modern* Eurasia* had an important bearing on contemporary politics, particularly in the developing world where "population growth and state crises ... remain companion phenomena."[3] Just like the absolutist agrarian states of the early modern period (roughly, the end of the fifteenth to the late eighteenth centuries), contemporary Third World* states with limited fiscal resources failed to provide for their rapidly expanding populations.

Academic Influences

Goldstone conducted his doctoral studies from 1979 to 1981 at Harvard University, where his dissertation advisor Theda Skocpol had a deep impact on his future work. In her seminal *State and Social Revolutions* (1979), this distinguished sociologist had argued that revolutions arise as much from the internal incapacities of states (or "state breakdown") as from violent opposition. As Skocpol famously wrote: "Revolutions are not made; they come,"[4] and her assertion that the structural weaknesses* of states (weaknesses in a state's ability to govern, expressed in military defeats, popular disorder, and so on) cause political and social revolutions influenced Goldstone's concept of state breakdown. But Goldstone stressed rapid population growth as the prime catalyst for revolutions—and this set his argument apart from Skocpol's, which attributed greater importance to class relations. So the originality of Goldstone's work stems from his focus on population escalation, which he believed was a necessary condition for state breakdown.

As a strong advocate of the macro-comparative* approach to the study of revolutions (a method of inquiry into structural patterns that lead to revolutions based on comparison of their outcomes), Skocpol also profoundly influenced Goldstone's methodology. In *State and Social Revolutions* she had sought to find a universal "logic of social revolutionary causes and outcomes" through comparing the French (1789–99),* Russian (1917)* and Chinese revolutions (1946–52).*[5] Goldstone adopted a similar approach in *Revolution and Rebellion*, comparing the causes behind the internal stress, disorder, and revolution suffered by Eurasia's agrarian bureaucratic regimes* from the seventeenth to the nineteenth centuries.

NOTES

1   Jack Goldstone, "Historical and Comparative Theory," in *Encyclopedia of Social Theory I*, ed. George Ritzer (Thousand Oaks, CA: SAGE Publications, 2005), 134–9.

2   Jack A. Goldstone, *Revolution and Rebellion in the Early Modern World* (Berkeley: University of California Press, 1991), 31.

3   Goldstone, *Revolution and Rebellion*, 475.

4   Theda Skocpol, *States and Social Revolutions: A Comparative Analysis of France, Russia and China* (Cambridge: Cambridge University Press, 1979), 17.

5   Skocpol, *States and Social Revolutions*, 292.

MODULE 3
THE PROBLEM

KEY POINTS

- One question has been central to political philosophy and sociology* since the nineteenth century: what causes revolutions?

- The comparative historical approach* to revolutions emerged as a dominant framework in sociology from the 1960s; this approach is used by social scientists to compare the characteristics of different societies in the same historical period.

- Goldstone adopted the comparative approach but gave greater attention to revolutions in Asia than his predecessors.

Core Question

Jack A. Goldstone's *Revolution and Rebellion in the Early Modern World* asks a simple question: which forces cause large groups of people to abandon their allegiance to a state? In other words, what causes revolutions? This question has been central to political philosophy since the nineteenth century, a period dubbed by the influential British historian Eric Hobsbawm* "The Age of Revolution."[1]

The question remains of vital importance to contemporary sociologists who seek to develop theoretical models that predict the sources and outcomes of political revolutions. The "sociology of revolutions" developed as an attempt to explain the "great" revolutions of the early twentieth century: the Russian Revolution,* in which the monarchy* was overthrown and replaced by a communist* government in 1917; the similar Chinese Revolution* of 1949; and the revolutions in the developing world that followed decolonization*

> ❝ Not the growth of capitalism, but a periodic, cyclic imbalance between population growth and inflexible economic and political systems, was responsible for the recurrent waves of state breakdown. ❞
>
> Jack A. Goldstone, *Revolution and Rebellion in the Early Modern World*

(the disintegration of European empires in the late nineteenth and twentieth centuries).

The question as to why revolutions occur is also of central importance to policymakers. As a result, sociologists of revolution have often sought to emphasize the contemporary, practical value of their work. In *Revolution and Rebellion*, Goldstone introduced his "political stress indicator" (PSI),* a mathematical model that sought to assess the likelihood of revolution in a given state. For Goldstone, the PSI not only allows sociologists to explain past revolutions, but also helps policymakers to predict the likelihood of future revolutions in areas of strategic national interest.

The Participants

Ever since the nineteenth century, the question as to why political and social revolutions occur has generated an enormous volume of discussion among historians and social scientists. The French Revolution* of 1789–99 and the Revolutions of 1848* (a spate of revolutions in northern and central Europe) prompted some of the earliest theories about their causes, notably from the nineteenth-century political thinkers Alexis de Tocqueville* of France and Karl Marx,* the influential German political philosopher whose analysis of class conflict, social history, and economics serves as the foundation for Marxist* theory.

In the twentieth century, another wave of revolutions in Russia, China, and the developing world sparked renewed interest in historical and sociological theories of revolution. In this regard, the comparative historical approach to revolutions pioneered in the 1960s by the social scientists Barrington Moore Jr.,* Charles Tilly,* and Theda Skocpol* proved especially crucial for modern sociologists. These thinkers argued that universal factors can be identified by comparing the revolutionary process across time and space.

Goldstone's work follows this tradition of sociological research in that he compares case studies of historical revolutions to develop generally applicable theories. However, he deviates from it in refusing to rely solely on Western European revolutions as the empirical basis for his work. Goldstone places such revolutions—notably the English* and French Revolutions—within a broader wave of rebellions that broke out across Europe and Asia between the seventeenth and nineteenth centuries. He rejects the view that Western Europe's revolutions were historically distinctive, or that they resulted from unique social, economic, and political structures—and therefore refutes the idea that Europe and Asia followed fundamentally different historical trajectories.

The Contemporary Debate

When Goldstone's *Revolution and Rebellion* was published, interpretations of early modern* revolutions were caught between two schools of thought. On the one hand, Marxist views continued to command support from some historians and sociologists. In the Marxist interpretation, the growth of capitalism* in Western Europe was the cause of early modern revolutions; the English and French Revolutions stemmed from a class struggle* between an emergent capitalist class* and members of the feudal* elite—those whose ownership of land conferred wealth, political influence, and social status. In these bourgeois* revolutions, an emerging capitalist class asserted its rights and political authority over the reactionary (conservative) nobility.

This interpretation had come under fire, however, from a generation of revisionist* historians (that is, historians who aimed to challenge orthodox interpretations) that included the British historians Alfred Cobban* and Richard Cobb* and the French historian François Furet,* who scrutinized orthodox Marxist accounts closely. Historians of the French Revolution, in particular, vociferously rejected the view that conflict between members of distinct classes caused early modern revolutions. Instead, conflicts and allegiances were seen to cut across supposedly rigid class boundaries. Revisionists tended to stress the accidental nature of revolutions, rather than long-term social transformations and class struggles.

But Goldstone charted a course between the Marxist and revisionist schools. Like the revisionists, he rejected the idea that the political history of early modern Europe amounted to a life-or-death battle between a rising capitalist class and entrenched nobility. Yet he also criticized the revisionist attempt to sweep away all ideas about the long-term economic and social causes of revolutions. Goldstone's theory of revolution therefore maintained continuity with Marxist accounts because it stressed large-scale structural factors and materialism* (the theory that changes in technological and productive capacity, rather than ideas or actions, are the primary driver of historical change). Further, Goldstone's account can be seen as an attempt to save these explanations of historical change from the onslaught of revisionism, while moving beyond the class-driven narratives of the Marxist school.

NOTES

1   Eric Hobsbawm, *The Age of Revolution: Europe 1789–1848* (UK: Abacus, US: Vintage, 1962).

MODULE 4
THE AUTHOR'S CONTRIBUTION

KEY POINTS

- Goldstone argues that European and Asian agrarian bureaucratic states* (states with agricultural economies and central governments) in the seventeenth and eighteenth centuries were structurally similar to each other, and succumbed to similar pressures.

- Goldstone offered a critique of the Eurocentrism* that dominated the history and sociology* of early modern* revolutions. (Eurocentrism is the tendency to view the world from the perspective of Western Europe, and to emphasize the exceptional character of the Western European experience).

- Goldstone's *Revolution and Rebellion* pushed the fields of global history* and demographic* history (that is, the history of changes in the makeup of a population) in new directions.

Author's Aims

Jack A. Goldstone wrote *Revolution and Rebellion in the Early Modern World* with the primary intent of refuting how the Marxist* school, with its emphasis on the conflict between different social classes, explained early modern revolutions, and to provide a new framework for understanding rebellion and revolution across Eurasia* from the seventeenth to nineteenth centuries. These instances included the English Revolution,* the French Revolution,* and the Revolutions of 1848* in northern and central Europe, as well as rebellions in China under the Qing* dynasty, in the nations subject to the Turkish Ottoman Empire,* and Japan of the Tokugawa* era.

> 66 Not the growth of capitalism, but a periodic, cyclic imbalance between population growth and inflexible economic and political systems, was responsible for the recurrent waves of state breakdown. 99
>
> *Jack A. Goldstone,* Revolution and Rebellion in the Early Modern World

In fact, Goldstone's theory of revolutions is resolutely anti-Marxist. It challenges the view that early modern revolutions resulted from class struggle* between members of emergent capitalist* and feudal* classes (those who enjoyed the status and wealth that came with the ownership of business, industry, or land in the late fifteenth to late eighteenth centuries). Instead, he provides an ecological* account of early modern revolutions that emphasizes how population dynamics strained the resources of agrarian bureaucratic states in early modern Eurasia. In Goldstone's account, long-term demographic trends—not conflict between social classes—drive historical change.

In his challenge to Marxist theories, Goldstone completely reassesses the impact of capitalism on early modern states. In the orthodox Marxist account, early modern states broke down under the aggression of capitalist producers who wrested political control from the feudal class.* But Goldstone counters that capitalism did not destabilize early modern states and lead them to the brink of revolution—in fact, it was the only economic system that could absorb population increases. Only highly productive capitalist forms of agriculture could provide states with the resources necessary to sustain long-term population growth. So the persistence of unproductive, feudal modes of economic organization, as opposed to the growth of capitalism, caused the wave of state breakdowns across Eurasia from 1500 to 1800.

Approach

Goldstone's approach to the study of early modern revolutions challenges the Eurocentrism inherent in Marxist accounts of seventeenth- and eighteenth-century revolutions. Marxists had emphasized the exceptional character of European revolutions, arguing that the rise of capitalism within Western Europe made its states uniquely prone to radical structural transformations. In contrast, political rebellions in Asia were seen to lack the dynamic force of capitalism, and were therefore dismissed as mere peasant* uprisings and dynastic changes. But Goldstone argues that Europe and Asia shared similar political and economic dynamics until the nineteenth century—and so challenges accounts that contrast Western dynamism with Eastern stagnation. By demonstrating the fundamental similarity of early modern European and Asian states, he asserts that revolutions and rebellions across Eurasia stemmed from similar origins.

Above all, he claims, the timing of demographic, climatic, and epidemiological* (disease-based) patterns gave Eurasia its unity in the early modern period. Population, climate, and disease exerted similar pressures on agrarian* states across the Eurasian continent, and placed constraints on raising the revenue needed to sustain and support expanding populations. Meanwhile, global demographic pressures— caused by declining mortality and increased fertility—also strained the financial resources of agrarian bureaucratic states. By making these connections, Goldstone provides a common frame for understanding patterns of political change in Western and non-Western societies.

Contribution in Context

Goldstone's *Revolution and Rebellion* can be positioned within two subfields of the humanities and social sciences: global history* (a discipline that seeks to examine patterns that emerge across cultures and geographical space) and demographic history.* By combining these two fields, Goldstone produced a novel account of how population dynamics affected political stability across Europe and Asia over two centuries. His book also contributed to a theoretical reorientation of these fields of knowledge.

Until the 1980s, global historians such as Joseph Needham,* Immanuel Wallerstein,* and Eric Jones* had been concerned with identifying the particular characteristics that allowed Europeans to triumph over other states and peoples of the world. Explaining the "rise of the West"* was a central preoccupation within the field, accomplished by determining the distinctive aspects of Western civilization that had ensured its success. Historians and sociologists had proposed a cluster of social, intellectual, economic, and political factors to explain Western Europe's unique historical trajectory. While Goldstone acknowledged the profound cultural differences between East and West, he forged a unique view of the early modern world that emphasized how European and Asian societies shared key similarities in their political and social structures.

While Goldstone's account of the early modern revolutions fits within an existing tradition of demographic history, it refrains from the determinism* that often plagued this field ("determinism" refers to the philosophical view that, given the prior presence of a certain set of variables, a determined set of events will unfold). For example, demographers have often asserted a simple equation between population growth, popular misery, and social unrest. In exploring the dynamic relationship between population trends, inflation,* state institutions, and economic policies, Goldstone emphasized that the impact of demographic trends on the stability of states depended on the decisions of key figures, and not on some set of universal demographic laws with a predetermined outcome. So his demographic/structural model of state breakdown helped to build a novel synthesis of demographic, political, and economic history.

SECTION 2
IDEAS

MAIN IDEAS

KEY POINTS

- The key themes in *Revolution and Rebellion in the Early Modern World* include state breakdown (identified by a government's inability to impose its will), fiscal crisis,* intra-elite conflict* (antagonisms between upwardly mobile, office-holding elites and traditional elites facing a downward trajectory), and mass-mobilization potential.

- For Goldstone, rapid demographic* growth (population growth) in the early modern period contributed to state breakdown by causing fiscal crises, intra-elite conflict and the potential for mass mobilization, or active civil unrest.

- Goldstone developed a mathematical formula, the "political stress indicator," to quantify the likelihood of revolutions.

Key Themes

Four core concepts are crucial for understanding Jack A. Goldstone's *Revolution and Rebellion in the Early Modern World*:

- State breakdown
- Fiscal crisis
- Intra–elite conflict
- Mass-mobilization potential.

"State breakdown" improves on the more diffuse, ill–defined terms "revolution" and "rebellion." State breakdown occurs when a centralized state* loses its capacity to impose its will and authority over a territory. Revolutions and rebellions are, then, instances of large–scale or total collapse of state authority.

> 66 If our model of the origins of the revolution is correct, we should find that the interaction product Ψ = Fiscal Distress X Mobility/Competition X Mass Mobilization Potential rises to a distinctive peak in the mid-seventeenth century, unmatched by a similar rise in either the sixteenth or eighteenth centuries. I have named this function by the Greek letter Ψ, serviceable as an acronym for 'political stress indicator,' hereafter psi. 99
>
> Jack A. Goldstone, *Revolution and Rebellion in the Early Modern World*

In a fiscal crisis, states lose the power to finance the operations required to maintain control over a territory. A fiscal crisis occurs when rapid population growth produces inflationary* pressures (roughly, the pressures of rising prices); combined with an unproductive agricultural sector and an inflexible taxation system, this places severe strains on a state's financial capacities.

In an intra-elite conflict, large numbers of elites defect from the existing regime. Those following the analytical approach of Karl Marx* (Marxism),* explained intra-elite conflict as the result of long-term struggles that pitted the commercial or capitalist* class against the landowning feudal* class. But Goldstone rejects this account of class struggle,* arguing instead that elites revolted because states failed to absorb them within their structure of patronage and reward. So intra-elite conflict was a direct result of demographically induced fiscal crises, as states lost the capacity to satisfy the ambitions of their elite.

The fourth core concept, mass-mobilization potential, refers to how easily the lower classes of a population can be drawn into elite-initiated revolts against the central state. When an increasing population puts pressure on natural resources, popular classes experience the greatest hardship, in the form of famines, unemployment, and poverty. However, the masses are only mobilized to voice their grievances when fiscal crises and intra-elite conflict produce a significant number of disaffected elites.

Exploring the Ideas

Goldstone knits a succinct theory of revolutions by examining how these demographically-induced factors—fiscal stress, intra-elite conflict and mass-mobilization potential—played out in early modern Eurasia.* In Goldstone's account, these necessary and sufficient conditions allowed state breakdown to occur.

Goldstone ties these three themes together in an elegant mathematical formula that he calls the "political stress indicator." Referred to by its acronym "psi" (and cleverly symbolized by the Greek letter of the same name), it relies on mathematical formulas that turn fiscal stress, intra-elite conflict, and mass mobilization potential into quantifiable variables. In each historical case of state breakdown, Goldstone uses the political stress indicator to measure how likely it was for revolution to have occurred. He then presents these calculations in graph form, demonstrating that periods rating high on the political stress indicator correlate with moments of state breakdown and revolution.

Goldstone uses the political stress indicator to great rhetorical* effect (that is, it becomes an important feature of an impressively articulated and persuasive argument). Readers are visually presented with seemingly irrefutable evidence for his theory of revolutions. The mathematical formulas also provide a common baseline for comparing the revolutions of England,* France,* the Turkish Ottoman Empire,* China,* and Japan.* And ultimately, the political stress indicator can also be used as a predictive tool that allows political scientists to measure and evaluate possible revolutionary outbreaks in fragile states.

Language and Expression

Goldstone's *Revolution and Rebellion* uses quantitative statistical modeling*— the collection and analysis of statistical information, an approach common to the social sciences but unusual for scholars in the humanities. Indeed, his quantitative approach to the study of revolutions has drawn criticism from noted historians such as the British scholar Lawrence Stone,* and may have slowed the gradual acceptance of Goldstone's work in the discipline. His critics maintained that revolutions and all forms of historical change are too complex, variable, and contingent (that is, they emerge from accidental circumstances) to reduce to a mathematical model—and that such attempts to do so produce illusory results. To be sure, Goldstone's numerical approach wielded power. But the mathematical aspect of his work provoked uneasiness among historians less willing to accept that statistics and a quantified sociology might be a useful way to arrive at "truths."

Goldstone's political stress indicator also leaves out ideology,* culture, and ideas as variables in the revolutionary equation (an ideology is a set of political beliefs that provide a framework for understanding the world). What is more, it would be difficult to imagine how to quantify these intangible (non-material) factors in a mathematical formula. The work by revisionist* historians of the French Revolution (that is, historians who deliberately challenge orthodox interpretations of historical events), including François Furet,* Lynn Hunt,* and Keith Michael Baker,* shows the crucial role of factors such as ideology, culture, and ideas in the lead-up to revolutions. Time and again, it has been shown that *how* people made sense of their experiences and grievances—through shared symbolism, language, and ideas—has a causal link to the outbreak of revolutions.

MODULE 6
SECONDARY IDEAS

KEY POINTS

- In *Revolution and Rebellion*, Goldstone argues that social scientists using algorithmic models* (statistical analysis as a predictive tool) could reliably predict revolutions.
- This neglected aspect of Goldstone's work is addressed to policymakers.
- Goldstone's work has contributed to a harmony between sociology* and public policy forecasting (the analysis of the effects of government policy).

Other Ideas

Jack A. Goldstone's account of state reconstruction in a post-revolutionary period makes up an important but secondary element of the wider thesis proposed in *Revolution and Rebellion in the Early Modern World*. Although principally concerned with the period leading to state breakdown, Goldstone briefly considers the factors that affect the reconstitution of states—the period of state rebuilding that makes up the final phase of revolutions, in which authority is stabilized and new sets of institutions are created.

While Goldstone denies that ideology* (a set of political beliefs that provide a framework for understanding the world) and culture play key roles in producing revolutions, he believes that these represent crucial components in the process of state reconstruction. The two forces provide the framework for elites to voice both their own grievances and those of the popular classes. Cultural and ideological forces also determine the shape of new institutions that replace those of the old regime.

> ❝ Macrosociology has unduly neglected the role of culture in shaping state structure and dynamics, particularly during periods of state crisis and reconstruction. Theories of social change must recognize that at some concrete historical junctures it is material forces, while at other such junctures it is cultural frameworks and ideologies, that play the dominant role in causing and directing change. ❞
>
> Jack A. Goldstone, *Revolution and Rebellion in the Early Modern World*

The transformative power Goldstone assigns to ideology and culture at the conclusion of his book comes as a surprise, given that his account is for the most part resolutely materialist* (that is, it focuses on quantifiable material factors). To an extent, this was his attempt to address criticisms of material determinism* (the philosophical view that, when of a certain set of variables is present, a determined set of events will unfold) leveled at the work of his intellectual mentor, Theda Skocpol,* in analyzing the revolutions in France,* Russia,* and China.* Goldstone's work provided a model that accommodated the role of culture within the revolutionary dynamics outlined in sociology.

Exploring the Ideas

For Goldstone, ideology and culture explain why state breakdowns had such radically different long-term structural results in Western and Eastern states. Still, he maintained that absolutist states* in Europe and Asia (states ruled by a single leader) had similar structures, and that the causes of their collapse were identical. Additionally, demographically★ induced fiscal crises* (difficulties concerning state revenue), intra-elite conflicts* (antagonisms between upwardly mobile office-holding elites and traditional elites facing downward social mobility) and mass mobilizations* (organized rebellion) affected them all. Yet one problem remains: how to account for the East/West divergence* in the nineteenth and twentieth centuries (the increasing military, technological, economic, and political supremacy of Western European nations and the United States from the nineteenth century onwards).

Goldstone solves this problem via the different cultural and ideological frameworks used by elites and popular groups to articulate sociopolitical grievances during a revolutionary crisis. He suggests that millenarian Christianity* (that is, belief that the end of the world is close) and eschatological* ideologies of progress (the belief that humanity is moving toward perfection) became embedded in post-revolutionary European political institutions—after being unleashed during revolutionary periods.

Then there is the legacy of "tradition-repudiating ideologies,"* which challenge old orthodoxies and social hierarchies while emphasizing that political institutions can be perfected. In post-breakdown European states, this acted as a defense against absolute authority and accounted for the emergence of dynamic political and economic institutions. This formed the foundation for representative government and led to the ascendency of capitalism* and free enterprise. In contrast, Asia's reconstructed states remained far more conservative because the ideologies that drove reconstruction were cyclical;* they called for the restoration of an old order purged of injustices, rather than the creation of a new one.

Overlooked

In the conclusion of *Revolution and Rebellion*, Goldstone assesses the potential applications of his findings to the prediction of future events—a point that has been largely neglected. As a result, many have overlooked the extent to which Goldstone meant his work to have an impact on public policy.

Indeed, Goldstone's political stress indicator (PSI)* was intended not only to explain historical events, but also to help policymakers forecast the outbreak of revolutions in fragile states.[1] He described his political stress indicator model as a "useful barometer … when the PSI levels are high, 'stormy weather,' politically speaking, is just over the horizon."[2] He believed that area specialists and revolution specialists could ultimately predict most revolutions if they worked together.

After the publication of *Revolution and Rebellion*, Goldstone advocated his political stress indicator model as a useful instrument of governance, and became deeply involved in public policy forecasting—two factors that should influence how we understand the historical importance of this text. The trajectory of his career reflects the increasing importance of quantitative sociological methods within the public policy sphere, and also the increasing reliance placed by intelligence professionals on statistical models developed by sociologists.

Since World War II* (1939–45), experts drawn from the social sciences have acted as consultants to policymakers and intelligence officials. But only in the past few decades have foreign policymakers systematically used algorithmic models* designed to predict state failure and political instability.[3] Goldstone was involved in the development of the PITF model (Political Instability Task Force,* a research project instigated by the US government to investigate state failure), which drew, in part, on the findings he presented in *Revolution and Rebellion*. His work not only reflects confidence in the usefulness and predictive capacity of analytical tools developed in the social sciences; it has also influenced public policy forecasting beyond any doubt.

NOTES

1   For the presentation of the political stress indicator model, see Jack A. Goldstone, *Revolution and Rebellion in the Early Modern World*, (Berkeley: University of California Press, 1991), 144–54.

2   Jack Goldstone, "Analyzing Revolutions and Rebellions: A Reply to the Critics," in *Debating Revolutions*, ed. Nikki R. Keddie (New York: New York University Press, 1995), 183.

3   Notable examples are the US Military's ACTOR (Analyzing Complex Threats for Operations and Readiness) model and the PITF (Political Instability Task Force) model, which Goldstone helped to develop. See Jack Goldstone, "Using Quantitative Models to Forecast Instability," *US Institute of Peace, Special Report 204* (March 2008).

MODULE 7
ACHIEVEMENT

KEY POINTS

- Non-European revolutions have received increasing attention since *Revolution and Rebellion in the Early Modern World*.
- Goldstone's work belongs to a "fourth wave" of sociologists* of revolution, which attributes increasing importance to culture and ideology.
- The field of world history has drawn on the insights of Goldstone's book.

Assessing the Argument

A decade before *Revolution and in the Early Modern World*, Jack A. Goldstone published the article "Theories of Revolution: The Third Generation" (1980), in which he divided twentieth-century sociologies of revolution into three categories:[1]

- Careful empirical investigations of revolutions (investigations founded on evidence verifiable by observation) that lacked a rigorous theoretical basis.
- Analyses of revolutions founded on Marxist*-inspired theories from political science, sociology, and psychology.
- More sophisticated models accommodating a greater number of variables than those of earlier class-based Marxist approaches (a category in which Goldstone placed his mentor, Theda Skocpol).*

In the twenty-first century, Goldstone's work is now widely regarded to have ushered in a "fourth generation" of revolutionary theory.[2] As the political scientist Eric Selbin* has written, Goldstone's work stimulated this new generation of theorists to move beyond the

> ❝ The fourth-generation scholars of revolution ... have moved beyond the smoldering structuralism of the third generation. Meaningful places for agents and the impact of culture have crept into the discussion. ❞
>
> Eric Selbin, *Revolution in the Real World*

state-centered, structural determinism* of third-generation theorists such as Skocpol. Structural determinism is the belief that social and economic structures are the sole and determining force of historical change, human behavior, culture, and ideas.

In retrospect, then, *Revolution and Rebellion* has been praised for integrating culture and ideology into sociological accounts of the revolutionary process. Sociologists—who were accustomed to state- and class-based structural accounts of revolutions—found a refreshing originality in Goldstone's approach to state construction. This stems from the importance that he granted to cultural and ideological* factors.

Achievement in Context

Another characteristic of this fourth generation of revolutionary theorists is that they have moved beyond studying only the great European social and political revolutions that rocked England, France and Russia. Goldstone's study of revolutions and rebellions in Eurasia* helped trigger new attempts to develop theories that embraced diverse cases, not only the list of classic (and popularly taught) revolutions. As a result, historical uprisings in the Middle East, South Asia, and East Asia—previously neglected by European sociologists—have received increasing attention.

Goldstone's comparative study of revolutions in early modern* Europe and Asia led him to suggest conclusions that would come to shape the core beliefs of the California School* (a term coined by Goldstone himself to refer to a group of academics, affiliated with universities in California, who challenged the view that Western Europe enjoyed some long-standing comparative advantage over Asia). These beliefs were first, that the so-called Great Divergence* between Europe and Asia (a socioeconomic shift that occurred between 1500 and 1800, which allowed Western European states to achieve global supremacy) occurred much later than was traditionally assumed; and second, that the causes of this late divergence occurred by chance— they were neither long-standing nor inherent to European civilization.

Such attempts to expose the accidental nature of European supremacy went against the dominant tradition in sociology that followed Karl Marx* and the pioneering sociologist Max Weber,*which assumed that it was the distinctive history of early modern Europe that had allowed it to develop the dynamic set of economic and political institutions that launched it on the path to global supremacy.

Limitations

Goldstone's *Revolution and Rebellion* has exerted a wide influence outside the immediate field of the study of revolutions within sociology. World history represents one area of study that has grown considerably since the book's publication. For the past two decades, scholars in this field have grappled with his theory of a demographically* driven global crisis that affected states across Eurasia in the early modern period. Regional case studies have been conducted to test whether it was a global ecological crisis that toppled absolutist agrarian regimes* (states with an agricultural economy, in which a single ruler holds all power) across early modern Europe and Asia.[3]

Taken together, these studies tend to confirm the theory of a global crisis, although Goldstone's demographic model has been subject to further examination and explanation. The world historian Geoffrey Parker,* for instance, has recently argued that climatic factors must be considered in explaining crises of the seventeenth century.[4] Overall, these findings square with Goldstone's claim that the root causes for the global revolutions were ecological. That *Revolution and Rebellion* sparked further interest in comparative world history* has been a welcome development for Goldstone, for he specifically sought to redefine the European experience of revolutions by setting them within a wider global context.

NOTES

1   Jack A. Goldstone, "Theories of Revolution: The Third Generation," *World Politics* 32 (1980): 425–53.

2   Eric Selbin, "Revolution in the Real World: Bringing Agency Back In," in *Theorizing Revolutions*, ed. John Foran. (New York: Routledge, 1997), 119.

3   Chester Dunning, "Does Jack Goldstone's Model of Early Modern State Crises Apply to Russia?" *Comparative Studies in Society and History* 39 (July 1997): 572–92; Sam White, *The Climate of Rebellion in the Early Modern Ottoman Empire* (Cambridge: Cambridge University Press, 2011).

4   Geoffrey Parker, "Crisis and Catastrophe: The Global Crisis of the Seventeenth Century Reconsidered," *American Historical Review* 113 (October 2008): 1053–79. This crisis refers to the political disturbances, driven by periods of famine and social unrest, in the seventeenth century.

MODULE 8
PLACE IN THE AUTHOR'S WORK

KEY POINTS

- The dominant focus of Goldstone's work has been to examine the relationship between political stability and demographic* trends.

- *Revolution and Rebellion* began Goldstone's career-long attempt to discover the origins of Western dominance.

- *Revolution and Rebellion* was his first work of detail and length, and quickly established him as a dominant figure in the discipline of sociology.*

Positioning

Although *Revolution and Rebellion in the Early Modern World* was Jack A. Goldstone's first scholarly work of such length and detail, it established his reputation as one of the leading sociologists of the late twentieth century. During the 1980s, he had published essays that examined the methods of comparative sociology,* and issued preliminary versions of his thesis in scholarly journals. But *Revolution and Rebellion* made his arguments visible to a wide community of social scientists. In 1993, the book was awarded the American Sociological Association Distinguished Scholarly Book Award,* one of the highest honors within the field of sociology.

Since the publication of this book, Goldstone has also turned his attention to the effects of long-term population trends on societies and states in the modern world; he has published a number of works over the past two decades about the threats posed to national security by population dynamics (patterns and trends in the constitution of populations and the environmental factors that influence them).[1] His

> ❝ Twenty-first century international security will depend less on how many people inhabit the world than on how the global population is composed and distributed: where populations are declining and where they are growing, which countries are relatively older and which are most youthful, and how demographics will influence population movements across regions. ❞
>
> Jack A. Goldstone, "The New Population Bomb"

most recent work warns of the dangers of global demographic imbalances* (disproportionately large numbers of young or elderly people in a population) and he has warned policymakers of the urgent need to address impending demographic catastrophe.[2]

Goldstone published much of his work on the contemporary relationship between national security and demographic trends in the wake of the terrorist attacks on the United States of September 11, 2001 ("9/11").* He argued, for instance, that rapid population growth in the Muslim world—and the resulting inability of states to provide employment, education, healthcare, and social services—has contributed to the political mobilization of disaffected Muslims by Islamic radicals.

Integration

Revolution and Rebellion anticipates much of Goldstone's later scholarship, which centers on how rapid population increases impede a given state's ability to maintain political stability, because they place stress on the resources required for steady functioning.[3] Goldstone continues to hold a view that emphasizes the long-term structural similarity of Europe and Asia, and sees the East/West divergence* as a phenomenon of the nineteenth century.

However, Goldstone has radically revised his original view that Europe's dynamism after 1800 was due to a secularized Christian cultural framework—that is, non-religious cultural habits and practices that have emerged from traditionally Christian societies—becoming embedded in the political institutions of nations following state breakdown. In his recent book *Why Europe? The Rise of the West in World History* (2008), Goldstone stresses the emergence of new methods of scientific investigation, and a key catalyst for the economic takeoff of the nineteenth century: the dense social networks of entrepreneurs and engineers that formed in eighteenth-century Britain.[4] This work can be seen as a logical sequel to *Revolution and Rebellion*. While his first book set out to demonstrate the fundamental similarity of East and West in the early modern* period, *The Rise of the West in World History* seeks to determine the critical factors that made divergence of these geopolitical regions possible.

Significance

Revolution and Rebellion exerted immediate influence on the discipline of sociology just a year after its publication, when the journal *Contemporary Sociology* held a symposium devoted to a critical appraisal of the work. The following year the journal *Contention* did the same; *Revolution and Rebellion* received acclaim from historical sociologists who welcomed the development of non-Marxist* structural theories to explain revolutionary conflict. The sociologist Randall Collins* praised the work as "state of the art" and "surely the best work on revolutions yet produced."[5] Collins commended Goldstone for supplanting the determinist,* class-driven Marxist accounts of revolutions with a sophisticated model that combined political, economic, social, cultural, and ideological* factors.

Goldstone's writings on the impact of current demographic trends on global security have also proved to be extremely influential in policy circles. His scholarship has informed the US intelligence community's forecasting of terrorism trends, and Goldstone has advised the United States Agency for International Development* and the World Bank* (an international monetary institution that provides loans to developing countries) on its policies towards fragile states at risk of ideological radicalization. His work has contributed to an increasing awareness of the impact of demographic trends on national and global political stability. As a consequence, Goldstone's ongoing analyses have had a far-reaching impact—not only within sociology as a discipline, but beyond the academic world and into the global political sphere as well.

NOTES

1   Jack Goldstone, "The New Population Bomb: Four Population Megatrends That Will Shape The Global Future," *Foreign Affairs* (Jan/Feb, 2010): 31–43; "Population Movements and Conflict," in *The International Studies Encyclopedia Vol. 9*, ed. Robert A. Denemark (Chichester, West Sussex: Wiley-Blackwell, 2010): 5822–35; "Demography and Security," in *Security and Development in Global Politics*, ed. Joanna Spear and Paul D. Williams (Washington, DC: Georgetown University Press, 2012), 271–90.

2   Goldstone, "The New Population Bomb," 31–43; "Population Movements and Conflict," 5822–35; "Demography and Security," 271–90.

3   Jack Goldstone, "Population Growth and Revolutionary Crises," in *Theorizing Revolutions*, ed. John Foran (London: Routledge, 1997), 102–20; "The Problem of the 'Early Modern' World," *Journal of the Economic and Social History of the Orient* 41 (1998): 249–84; "Population and Progress in the Middle Ages," *Population and Development Review* 27 (2001): 585–96; "Rethinking Revolutions: Integrating Origins, Processes, and Outcomes," *Comparative Studies of South Asia, Africa, and the Middle East* 29 (2009): 8–32.

4   Jack Goldstone, *Why Europe? The Rise of the West in World History, 1500-1800* (New York: McGraw-Hill, 2008).

5   Randall Collins, "Maturation of the State-Centered Theory of Revolution and Ideology," *Sociological Theory* 11 (March 1993): 118.

SECTION 3
IMPACT

THE FIRST RESPONSES

KEY POINTS

- Goldstone's *Revolution and Rebellion* was criticized for being too deterministic* (that is, for holding the view that if a certain set of variables is in place, a determined set of events will unfold); for marginalizing the role of culture and ideology* in revolutions; and for relying on quantitative modeling* (predictive models based on statistical measurements).

- Goldstone maintained that structural factors were the prime movers in causing revolutions.

- *Revolution and Rebellion* was received much more positively among sociologists* than historians.

Criticism

Jack A. Goldstone's *Revolution and Rebellion in the Early Modern World* prompted widespread debate within the humanities and social sciences. Critiques of his methodology attacked the deterministic and monocausal* (attributable to a single cause) nature of his theory of revolutions. In a respectful but pointed appraisal of the work, the noted sociologist Charles Tilly* questioned the value of "singular models of revolution" such as Goldstone's.[1]

Tilly rejects the notion that revolutions can be explained in terms of "necessary and sufficient conditions" such as fiscal crises* (issues concerning a state's finances), intra-elite conflict* (conflicts caused by shifting allegiances among the political class) and mass-mobilization potential* (the potential for organized rebellion).[2] Further, he argues that sociologists must explain the variable conditions under which

> 66 What is wholly unacceptable is to use a pseudo-scientific* methodology like a political stress indicator to solve a complex political issue. 99
>
> Lawrence Stone, "The Stress Revolution: Lawrence Stone replies"

revolutions occur, rather than develop singular models to describe them. So Tilly's response to *Revolution and Rebellion* raised a crucial question for sociologists: can the dynamics of revolutions be reduced to a universal model, or are they unique phenomena beyond the scope of mechanical sociological laws?

Meanwhile, some historians critiqued Goldstone's work by pointing out the pitfalls of relying on population data and that of monetary trends at a time when such measurements were notoriously unreliable. Lawrence Stone,* the eminent historian of the English Revolution,* condemned Goldstone's attempt to turn "fuzzy and unreliable data into hard statistics and graphs"—characterizing it as a gross "misuse of the scientific method of quantification." His criticism of Goldstone's faith in graphs and statistics summarizes the aversion many historians feel for reducing qualitative historical change to quantitative form. Stone then went further, mocking Goldstone's political stress indicator,* which provides a mathematical formula for measuring the likelihood of a revolution. He slammed it as a creation of fantasy, "about as real as a unicorn."[3]

Responses

In the years following *Revolution and Rebellion*, Goldstone defended his ideas in a number of forums. He replied to Lawrence Stone's criticism the following year in the *New York Review of Books*,[4] defending the utility of his political stress indicator (psi). The psi, he maintained, was a powerful analytical tool that allowed historical sociologists to measure the causal importance of numerous structural factors in producing revolutions. Unfortunately, Goldstone did not address the core of Stone's critique: that the political stress indicator was "a pseudo-scientific* methodology" that left readers "without the faintest idea of how much weight he has given to the various factors and why, in the compilation of the graph."[5] In the subsequent dialogue, Stone replied that given Goldstone's apparent inability to provide a justification for the political stress indicator, it was "unlikely that historians will take his work very seriously."[6]

Goldstone issued another response to his critics in a special issue of the social scientific journal *Contention*, subsequently reprinted in the volume *Debating Revolutions*. Goldstone's reply to Charles Tilly revealed that the two scholars held profoundly different assumptions regarding the nature of revolutions. Tilly viewed them as too particular, contingent (dependent on accidental circumstances), and variable to be explained by the kind of single-cause models developed by Goldstone.[7] In contrast, Goldstone claims that while revolutions are variable, they are also homogenous in structure. In other words, while no revolution is the same as any other, an identifiable set of common factors can explain and predict these uprisings. For Goldstone, the proof lies in the political stress indicator, which demonstrates that revolutions can be reliably predicted—and that they follow a singular set of universally stable laws.

Conflict and Consensus

Scholars who deplored Goldstone's marginalization of culture and ideology in the revolutionary process also questioned his ideas. The causal role of these two forces in producing revolutions had been stressed in the 1980s by François Furet,* Lynn Hunt,* and Keith Michael Baker* in their revisionist* accounts of the French Revolution.* Jeffrey Wasserstrom* followed their lead in his essay "Bringing Culture Back In and Other Caveats: A Critique of Jack

Goldstone's Recent Essays on Revolutions." He challenged Goldstone's insistence that ideology and culture do not play a role in determining the outbreak of revolutions.[8] For Wasserstrom, structural explanations can only account for the likelihood that states will suffer breakdown; ideologies and culture have to be considered in accounts of why and how groups of people decide to attack existing institutions. So he sees no need to create a hierarchy of causes; instead he urges historians and sociologists to investigate the relationship between structural, ideological, and cultural factors.

Goldstone also defended himself against claims that his theory of revolutions is crudely materialistic* (that is, founded on the belief that changes in material factors such as technology and production, rather than ideas or human action, are the primary drivers of historical change). He pointed out that his model grants a moderately important role to culture and ideology—if not in causing revolutions, then in determining the shape taken by states in the post-revolutionary reconstruction phase.

But he refused to back down from his core claim—that the causes of revolution are purely structural, and not cultural or ideological. He defended this on the basis that he had found "no empirical correlation* between specific kinds of culture, or specific changes in culture, and state breakdown."[9] Yet it is hard to see how culture and ideology— intangible factors, after all—could be submitted to this empirical examination. As a result, Goldstone's rebuttal exposes the limitations of his reliance on mathematical modeling* and quantitative methods. That is, any factors that he could not properly quantify in the form of numerical data were simply dismissed as lacking causal force. So Goldstone fails to address those historians and sociologists who claim that culture and ideology are important components in revolutionary change. Put another way: Goldstone's trust in numbers has not earned him the trust of all his colleagues.

NOTES

1   Charles Tilly, "The Bourgeois Gentilhommes of Revolutionary Theory," in *Debating Revolutions*, ed. Nikki R. Keddie (New York: New York University Press, 1995), 136–45.

2   Tilly, "The Bourgeois Gentilhommes of Revolutionary Theory," 136–45.

3   Lawrence Stone, "The Revolution Over the Revolution," *New York Review of Books*, June 11, 1992.

4   Jack Goldstone, "The Stress Revolution," *New York Review of Books*, April 22, 1993.

5   Stone, "The Revolution Over the Revolution."

6   Lawrence Stone, "Lawrence Stone replies," *New York Review of Books*, April 22, 1993.

7   Tilly, "The Bourgeois Gentilhommes of Revolutionary Theory," 136–145.

8   Jeffrey Wasserstrom, "Bringing Culture Back In and Other Caveats: A Critique of Jack Goldstone's Recent Essays on Revolution," in *Debating Revolutions*, ed. Nikki R. Keddie (New York: New York University Press, 1995), 155–78.

9   Jack Goldstone, "Analyzing Revolutions and Rebellions: A Reply to the Critics," in *Debating Revolutions*, ed. Nikki R. Keddie (New York: New York University Press, 1995), 186.

MODULE 10
THE EVOLVING DEBATE

KEY POINTS

- Goldstone's *Revolution and Rebellion* challenged existing theories of Western modernization* (the process through which a society passes from "traditional" to "modern.")

- Goldstone was a founding member of the "California School"* (academics affiliated with universities in California who challenged the view that Western Europe held a long-standing comparative advantage over Asia).

- *Revolution and Rebellion* was a seminal contribution to the "Great Divergence"* debate (discussion on the causes and timing of the social distinctions between Asia and Europe).

Uses and Problems

One of the biggest challenges Jack A. Goldstone posed to historians and sociologists in *Revolution and Rebellion in the Early Modern World* was to revise existing theories about Western modernization. In claiming that Europe and Asia were structurally similar until the nineteenth century, Goldstone also rejected other theories that attributed their divergence to long-term internal factors. In many ways this argument was secondary to Goldstone's larger project—mostly because he felt that assumptions of structural unity in Eurasia* over the early modern* period required little defense. Yet inadvertently, this has become one of the most contentious claims made in *Revolution and Rebellion* and continues to fuel debates within the humanities and social sciences.

Prior to *Revolution and Rebellion*, few challenged the view that Western Europe's rise to global hegemony (dominance) began in the early modern period. Scholars worked from this assumption and

> 66 Why did the first breakthrough of the Malthusian ceiling—the tension between population and available resources—occur in Western countries, to begin with in Britain, and not in other parts of the world? That of course is a classic problem. With the emergence of the so-called California School of economic history, however, it has been posed in a new way and framed explicitly in a context of global comparisons and connections. 99
>
> Peer Vries, "The California School and Beyond: How to Study the Great Divergence"

debated which factors were most responsible for the ascent of Western European powers. The factors considered included the rise of capitalism,* the scientific revolution (the development of physics, medicine, biology, astronomy, and mathematics in the early modern period), the emergence of representative forms of government (law-making bodies in which members are elected to serve the people), and the predominance of monotheistic and non-animistic religions (religions founded on a single god and in which spirits are not believed to reside in natural forces, animals, or objects).

Revolution and Rebellion changed the rules of the game by making an early modern split between East and West something to prove rather than assume. Goldstone disputed Eurocentric* accounts, in which the primacy of European history, values, and perspectives were assumed, and which contrasted Western dynamism with Eastern stagnation; he argued instead that Europe and Asia shared political and economic dynamics for three centuries.

Schools of Thought
Revolution and Rebellion is now viewed, in retrospect, as a seminal contribution to the "Great Divergence" debate concerning the timing

and causes of the differences between Europe and Asia. Its seminal thesis, later championed by the academics of the California School, held that no significant split existed between the political and economic dynamics found in Europe and Asia prior to the nineteenth century. Members of the California School—which includes the economic historians Roy Bin Wong* and Andre Gunder Frank,* and the historian Kenneth Pomeranz*—recognize the cultural and institutional differences within Eurasia, but they also believe that East and West shared similar political and economic structures. In short, the unifying factor in Eurasia was that agrarian bureaucratic states* (to use a term coined in *Revolution and Rebellion*, designating states with agricultural economies and active central government) managed the territories of the landmass.

So *Revolution and Rebellion* provides a jumping-off point for rethinking recent narratives of European modernization. The California School has tackled one of the oldest problems in social theory—the rise of the West*—but in a radically new analytical framework that traces its embryonic stage to the publication of *Revolution and Rebellion*. This framework treats Asia and Europe symmetrically: that is, it assumes no innate, long-term structural or cultural differences or advantages between the two, focusing instead on other, accidental and geographical, factors.

In Current Scholarship

Revolution and Rebellion's early statement of the thesis that shaped the core beliefs of the California School was this: the so-called Great Divergence between Europe and Asia occurred much later than traditionally assumed, and the causes were fortuitous rather than long-standing and endogenous* (that is, originating from within the society or state).

Yet while contemporary proponents of the California School agree on the basic principle of Eurasian similarity set out in the

Revolution and Rebellion, they depart from Goldstone's explanation for the later divergence. On this point, the unity of the California School breaks down. Some, such as Andre Gunder Frank, point to soil exhaustion* in China as a key factor; others, such as Kenneth Pomeranz and Roy Bin Wong, stress the importance of geographical chance, such as the availability of large coal deposits in Britain.[1]

Beginning as a factional group of academics on the west coast of the United States, the California School today attracts a large number of followers who continue to question the old commonly held view of early modern Europe as a dominant, advanced civilization destined for global superiority in the eighteenth and nineteenth centuries. In short, these modern disciples seek to overturn the paradigm—that is, the intellectual framework inside which evidence is interpreted—that prevailed at the time *Revolution and Rebellion* was published. Of course, these claims have not gone unchallenged, but proponents of the old orthodoxy have been pushed onto the defensive.[2] So in this sense, *Revolution and Rebellion* changed the debate surrounding the socioeconomic history of the early modern period.

NOTES

1   Andre Gunder Frank, *ReOrient: Global Economy in the Asian Age* (Berkley: University of California Press, 1998); Roy Bin Wong, *China Transformed: Historical Change and the Limits of European Experience* (Ithaca: Cornell University Press, 1997); Kenneth Pomeranz, *Great Divergence: China, Europe and the Making of the World Economy* (Princeton: Princeton University Press, 2000).

2   The most vocal opponent of this school is the sociologist Joseph M. Bryant. See Joseph M. Bryant, "The West and the Rest Revisited: Debating Capitalist Origins, European Colonialism, and the Advent of Modernity," *Canadian Journal of Sociology* 31 (2006): 403–44.

MODULE 11
IMPACT AND INFLUENCE TODAY

KEY POINTS

- Goldstone's work remains a classic contribution to the "Great Divergence"* debate.
- Goldstone's argument for the structural similarity of Europe and Asia has been subjected to empirical* scrutiny.
- In recent years, sociologists* have argued for a return to Eurocentric* accounts of the Western rise to global dominance (that is, accounts that assume the primacy of European experience, perspectives, or history).

Position

Jack A. Goldstone's *Revolution and Rebellion in the Early Modern World* represents one of the first works to bring comparative history* methods to bear on the question of East/West divergence.* Goldstone argues that any comparison of Eastern and Western absolutist monarchies* from 1500 to 1800 reveals remarkable similarities rather than pronounced differences. The thesis of a broad structural similarity before about 1800 has since led to attempts to answer a puzzling question: how exactly did Europe move ahead of the East so rapidly in the first half of the nineteenth century?

Revolution and Rebellion was partly responsible for a factional split among global historians and theorists of European modernization. The current intellectual debate divides the proponents of long-term, endogenous* (internal, native) causes of European dominance—most prominently the sociologist and historian Joseph M. Bryant*—and those such as Kenneth Pomeranz* and Roy Bin Wong,* who, being revisionists,* challenge orthodox interpretations of history by arguing

> **❝** I would never claim that European superiority 'came out of nowhere' in a sudden flash. But I strongly claim that it did not come out of long-standing commercial, technological, or material superiority. **❞**
>
> Jack Goldstone, "Reply to Bryant"

for short-term, incidental causes. For Pomeranz and Wong, it was the strategic availability of coal in Britain that allowed it to forge ahead of the rest of Europe and Asia, not any longstanding structural superiority. While members of the revisionist school continue to argue among themselves about the specific contingent factors that caused the rapid takeoff after 1800, they nevertheless share a commitment to an analytical framework first put forward in *Revolution and Rebellion*.

Interaction

The empirical basis for Goldstone's Eurasian similarity thesis has been scrutinized over the past two decades. Some historians contest the data used to argue for similar levels of economic productivity and standards of living in early modern Europe and Asia. Economists and comparative historians are now empirically testing the validity of claims made by revisionist historians and sociologists. Many of the findings suggest that earlier claims of East/West parity are exaggerated, if not completely invalid. For instance, the British economic historian Stephen Broadberry* and the British historian Bishnupriya Gupta* conclude, based on their study of wage rates in Europe and Asia from 1500 to 1800, that "advanced parts of Asia in 1800 should be seen as on the same developmental level as the stagnating parts of the European periphery."[1]

Yet the amount of empirical research generated to test the thesis of late divergence, first put forward in *Revolution and Rebellion*, is remarkable. An entire recent issue of *The Journal of Economic History*** was devoted to presenting the latest data. Regardless of whether the Eurasian similarity thesis will stand the test of such scrutiny, it has provided an impetus for Anglo-American scholars to study early modern* Asian economic history.

The Continuing Debate

In *Revolution and Rebellion*, Goldstone challenged the narrative of long-term, structural divergence—and his 1991 book continues to fuel debate today. Joseph M. Bryant* offered a recent defense of the Eurocentric consensus in his provocative essay "The West and the Rest Revisited: Debating Capitalist Origins." Bryant attacks the model of historical causation put forward by Goldstone and the revisionists as an "ontological impossibility" (that is, fundamentally impossible according to philosophy's teachings about the very nature of being) and "logically indefensible."[2] In Bryant's view the "eagerness to provincialize the European narrative by identifying purported structural similarities" between Europe and Asia has clouded the better judgment of revisionists such as Goldstone.[3]

Additionally, Bryant believes that the European economic takeoff in the nineteenth century was so rapid that only deep-rooted historical causes could have produced it. Bryant concludes with an appeal to the authority of the founders of structuralist sociology (that is, approaches that seek to identify and analyze structures such as class): "Their European provenance notwithstanding, the lessons of Marx and Weber still apply."[4] For Bryant, contingency—that is, the role of the accidental—is not enough to replace multi-layered structural accounts of historical change. The continuing debate between Goldstone and Bryant is widely relevant within the humanities and social sciences— for at its heart lies spirited disagreement about the very nature of historical change.[5]

NOTES

1   Stephen Broadberry and Bishnupriya Gupta, "The Early Modern Great
    Divergence: Wages, Prices and Economic Development in Europe and Asia,
    1500-1800," *Economic History Review* 59 (2006): 2.

2   Joseph M. Bryant, "The West and the Rest Revisited: Debating Capitalist
    Origins, European Colonialism, and the Advent of Modernity," *Canadian
    Journal of Sociology* 31 (2006): 437–8.

3   Joseph M. Bryant, "A New Sociology for a New History? Further Critical
    Thoughts on the Eurasian Similarity and Great Divergence Theses,"
    Canadian Journal of Sociology 22 (Spring 2008): 160.

4   Bryant, "The West and the Rest," 440. Both Marx and Weber had claimed
    that the development of capitalism in Western Europe had taken these
    societies on a historical trajectory radically different from those of non-
    European societies.

5   A point made by Goldstone in his reply to Bryant. See Jack Goldstone,
    "Capitalist Origins, the Advent of Modernity, and Coherent Explanation:
    A Reply to Joseph M. Bryant," *Canadian Journal of Sociology* 33 (2008):
    119–33.

WHERE NEXT?

KEY POINTS

- Goldstone's ecological* approach to the study of revolutions will continue to wield influence.

- Historians now widely agree that environmental factors constrain states' abilities to govern.

- Goldstone's demographic* account of revolutions in the early modern* world remains a crucial contribution to the sociology* of revolutions.

Potential

Jack A. Goldstone's *Revolution and Rebellion in the Early Modern World* revealed that the main threats to early modern states were ecological: variations in disease patterns, and mortality and fertility rates, could severely destabilize a nation's capacity to maintain order. The ecological model of state breakdown proposed by Goldstone in *Revolution and Rebellion* is likely to receive further interest from future generations of scholars grappling with the problem of shrinking environmental resources—made all the more fragile and scarce by a global population that hit more than seven billion in 2015. Growing public concern about a precarious natural environment and decreasing natural resources in the past decades has provided, if nothing else positive, a boon to environmental studies.

It is probable that Goldstone's ecological model of revolutions will receive further scholarly attention. Indeed, it appears that this process has already begun. A great amount of work is currently examining how environmental factors affect states' ability to maintain order. This work follows Goldstone in investigating the dynamic interrelationship

> **❝** The Scottish Revolution thus offers a perfect vindication of Voltaire's thesis that rebellions arose during the mid-seventeenth century through a fatal synergy between the government, religion, and climate. Charles's insistence on creating 'one uniform course of government in, and through our whole monarchy,' especially in matters of religion, coupled with the Little Ice Age, led to state collapse. **❞**
>
> Geoffrey Parker, "Crisis and Catastrophe"

between ecological, political, and economic structures. The British historian Geoffrey Parker,* for instance, has recently built on Goldstone's thesis to argue that both climate and population changes—factors relevant in the twenty-first century—caused the "global crisis" of the seventeenth century.[1]

Future Directions

Environmental transformations received little attention in *Revolution and Rebellion*, despite Goldstone's claim that he provided an "ecological" account of revolutions. He primarily restricted his ecological variables to disease and mortality rates, while assuming that a stagnant but stable agricultural sector would eventually be outstripped by population increases. What he left out of the account, though, was the variability of natural environmental factors such as soil exhaustion* (when soil becomes barren due to over-farming), climate pattern change and diminishing natural resources—and ultimately, their overarching effect on political structures. Global epidemiological trends* (trends in infectious disease) represented just one of many environmental factors that affected the stability of early modern states.

A recent case study of the Ottoman Empire* crisis by the historian Sam White* drew inspiration from Goldstone's ecological account of state breakdown—but it also emphasized the importance of a changing climate, natural disasters, and agricultural epidemics in eroding the Ottoman state.[2] For White, the "Little Ice Age,"* a period of cooling global temperatures that extended from the medieval period to the eighteenth century, represented "the underlying cause of perhaps the worst crisis in Ottoman history."[3] Today, the impending threat of resource scarcity, environmental instability, and increasing population pressures may endanger us all—and this shadow alone is likely to sustain interest in Goldstone's thesis as presented in *Revolution and Rebellion*.

Summary

Revolution and Rebellion in the Early Modern World is a classic work of historical sociology and a seminal text in the comparative sociology of revolutions.* In this work, Goldstone developed a novel theory of revolutions that emphasized the crucial role of demographic trends, and how they destabilized agrarian bureaucratic states* across early modern Eurasia.* He therefore contested the dominant theories presented by Marxist* historians and sociologists, whose accounts of revolutions stressed class struggle;* instead, he emphasized the interplay of structural and ecological factors.

Perhaps Goldstone's most provocative claim was that the European revolutions made up part of a broader Eurasian wave of state crises. By arguing that a common set of demographic trends impinged on states across Eurasia—and that those states were structurally similar—he undermined the assumption that early modern Europe possessed a distinct set of institutions and social structures that launched it on the path to global dominance and modernity. European revolutions, in his account, were not violent ruptures that allowed for the breakthrough of new modes of production and social organization. Rather, they

were instances of state failure broadly characteristic of all agrarian*
states in early modern Eurasia.

Revolution and Rebellion has inspired a generation of scholars to
revise old assumptions about the structural uniqueness of early
modern Europe—and to rethink and revise inherited narratives of
European modernization.* This project continues in the work of the
California School,* of which Goldstone was a founding member.
And in the years since its 1991 release, the book has succeeded
enormously in overturning old certainties about the course of Western
European development. In that sense, *Revolution and Rebellion*, for all
its continued influence, has already fostered a revolution for the
history books.

NOTES

1   Geoffrey Parker, "Crisis and Catastrophe: The Global Crisis of the
    Seventeenth Century Reconsidered," *American Historical Review* 113
    (October 2008): 1053–79.

2   Sam White, "The Little Ice Age Crisis of the Ottoman Empire: A Conjuncture
    in Middle East Environmental History," in *Water on Sand: Environmental
    Histories of the Middle East and North Africa*, ed. Alan Mikhail (Oxford:
    Oxford University Press, 2012), 72.

3   White, "The Little Ice Age Crisis," 72.

GLOSSARY

GLOSSARY OF TERMS

9/11: the terrorist attacks of September 11, 2001, that destroyed the World Trade Center in New York and also damaged the Pentagon in Washington DC.

Absolutist agrarian states: states ruled by a single leader, which derive the majority of their revenues from agricultural production.

Absolutist monarchy: a political system in which a monarch (king or queen) has complete control of the state.

Agrarian: to do with agriculture.

Agrarian bureaucratic regimes: the large-scale centralized, hereditary monarchies that controlled much of the Eurasian continent between 1500 and 1800, and whose primary tax base was the agricultural sector.

Algorithmic models: tools used by social scientists to predict the course of future events through statistical analysis.

American Sociological Association Distinguished Scholarly Book Award: a prize awarded annually since 1986 by the American Sociological Association.

Bourgeois: a term for the middle classes, particularly used to describe those with conservative attitudes who want to maintain the status quo and protect their own interests.

California School: a term coined by Jack A. Goldstone to refer to a group of academics mainly affiliated with universities in California. Its members challenge the view that Western Europe had an intrinsic long-standing advantage over the East that stretched back to the later Middle Ages.

Capitalism: an economic system characterized by the private ownership of capital assets and property, in which prices for goods and labor are, in theory, freely determined by competition and demand.

Capitalist class: members of the class that derive their revenues from investments in manufacturing and trade.

Centralized state: a government that holds executive power over smaller units of authority that are considered dependent.

Central Intelligence Agency (CIA): the principal intelligence-gathering institution in the United States.

Chinese Revolution (1949): a revolution that led to the foundation of the Communist People's Republic of China, led by Mao Zedong.

Class struggle: a concept central to Marxist thinking that refers to the tensions and antagonisms resulting from the competing interests of members of different socioeconomic classes.

Communism: a form of government based on the anti-capitalist philosophy of Karl Marx, in which, theoretically, the ultimate aim is to establish a classless society where the means of production are communally owned by all citizens.

Comparative history: a methodological approach used by social scientists that compares the characteristics of different societies over the same historical period.

Comparative sociology: an approach used by social scientists to compare the characteristics of different societies.

Comparative sociology of revolutions: a scholarly field that attempts to discern general structural patterns that lead to the outbreak of revolutions by comparing their outcomes across time and space.

Conflict theory: a subfield of sociology that examines how material, political, and social inequalities produce conflicts between different social groups.

Cyclical ideologies: ideologies that see human history as a continuous process of birth and decay.

Decolonization: the disintegration of European empires in the late nineteenth and twentieth centuries.

Demography: the statistical study of human population trends.

Demographic history: the study of human population trends in the past.

Demographic imbalances: the situation in populations that have disproportionately large numbers of young or elderly people.

Determinism: the philosophical position that a determined set of events will unfold, given the prior presence of a certain set of variables.

Early modern: a term first used by historians in the 1940s to designate the unique features of a post-medieval and pre-modern historical period (roughly the end of the fifteenth century to the end of the eighteenth century).

East/West divergence: the increasing military, technological, economic, and political supremacy of Western European nations and the United States from the nineteenth century onwards.

Ecology: the study of the interaction of human and non-human organisms with their natural environments.

Empirical: founded on the analysis of information verifiable by observation.

Empirical correlation: the interdependence between variables.

Endogenous factors: characteristics that originate from within an organism, society, or culture.

English Revolution (1642–51): a period of armed conflict that pitted supporters of the English Parliament against royalist forces who supported the English monarch Charles I.

Epidemiological trends: the incidence of disease across geographical space.

Epidemiology: the study of disease and health, including what causes disease and how it spreads.

Eschatological ideologies: belief systems that see the unfolding of human history as an evolution toward an ultimate point of perfection.

Eurasia: the landmass on which the continents of Europe and Asia are situated.

Eurocentrism: the tendency to view the world from the perspective of Western Europe, and to emphasize the exceptional character of the

Western European experience.

Feudal class: members of the class that derive their revenues from rents provided by agricultural tenants.

Feudalism: an economic system that flourished during the Middle Ages and early modern period based on the holding of agricultural land in exchange for rents, labor, and services.

Fiscal crises/stress: the difficulties faced by states in raising sufficient revenues to finance their operations.

French Revolution: a period of social upheaval between 1789 and 1799 that witnessed the collapse of the Bourbon monarchy, and the establishment of a republican government.

Global history: a discipline that seeks to examine common patterns that emerge across cultures and geographical space.

Great Divergence: a term first coined by the political scientist Samuel Huntington (1927–2008). It refers to a supposed long-term socioeconomic shift that occurred between 1500 and 1800 and which allowed Western European states to achieve global supremacy.

Historical demography: the study of human population trends in the past.

Historical sociology: a branch of sociology that examines the historical development of social structures and institutions.

Ideology: a set of political beliefs that provide a framework for understanding the world.

Industrial Revolution: the period of technological innovation and transformations in the modes of industrial production between about 1760 and 1840.

Inflation: a sustained increase in the price of goods, leading to a reduction in purchasing power.

Intra-elite conflict: antagonisms between upwardly mobile office-holding elites and traditional elites who face downward social mobility due to a lack of opportunities within the patronage structure of cash-strapped states.

Iranian Revolution: a revolution that led to the overthrow of the US-backed Pahlavi Dynasty in 1979 and the founding of an Islamic republic led by the religious leader Ayatollah Khomeini.

Journal of Economic History: a leading academic journal within the field of economic history, published since 1941.

Little Ice Age: a period of cooling of global temperatures that occurred at the end of the medieval period until the eighteenth century.

McCarthyism: a period of heightened fear of communism in the United States between 1950 and 1954. The term derives from the anti-communist crusade led by Wisconsin senator Joseph McCarthy.

Malthusianism: ideas derived from the writings of the pioneering English demographer Thomas Malthus (1766–1834), and more generally applied to scholarship that investigates the relationship between social stability and population trends.

Marxism: a body of thought inspired by the writings of Karl Marx that emphasizes the role of class struggle as an engine of historical change.

Mass-mobilization potential: the likelihood that the popular classes will be mobilized into political action by disaffected traditional elites.

Mathematical modeling: the use of mathematical language and concepts to make predictions about events and behavior.

Material determinism: a theory that marginalizes the importance of human will and agency, asserting that material conditions (in technology and production, for example) drive historical change.

Materialism: the theory that history is driven by changes in material conditions—technological and productive capacity, for example—rather than ideas or human agency.

Millenarian Christianity: the belief in the imminent coming of the apocalypse, or the end of the world. Goldstone argued that apocalyptic thinking allowed Europeans to conceive of the secular and progressive movement of history.

Ming dynasty: the ruling dynasty of China from 1368–1644.

Modernization: a process through which a society passes from a "traditional" to a "modern" society.

Monarchy: a system of government in which a monarch (king or queen) holds power.

Monocausal: an adjective describing explanations of phenomena that rely on a single cause.

Nicaraguan Revolution: a revolution that occurred in 1979 when the Sandinista National Liberation Front deposed the Nicaraguan dictator Anastasio Somoza Debayle, ushering in a decade of political and economic reforms along socialist lines

Ontology: the examination of the nature of being, or existence.

Ottoman Empire: an imperial dynasty that ruled Anatolia (present-day Turkey) and vast stretches of territory around the Mediterranean Sea from 1453 until its dissolution in 1922.

Peasants: members of a traditional class of farmers who are often poor, of low social status, and dependent on landholding agrarian elites.

Periodization: the division of historical epochs along a timeline.

Political Instability Task Force: a United States government-sponsored research project founded to analyze factors leading to state failure.

Political stress indicator (psi): a mathematical formula developed by Jack A. Goldstone that turns fiscal stress, intra-elite conflict and mass mobilization potential into quantifiable variables. It is used to determine the likelihood of contemporary or historical state failures.

Pseudo-scientific: the quality of appearing to be scientific, while in fact having no basis in science.

Qing China/Qing dynasty: the Qing dynasty was China's last imperial dynasty, which ruled from 1644 to 1911. It was overthrown by Chinese nationalists, who established a new government on republican principles.

Quantitative modeling/quantitative statistical modeling: the collection and analysis of statistical information.

Revisionism: challenges to orthodox interpretations of historical events. In the historiography of the French Revolution, revisionists sought to counter the class-driven narrative of Marxist historians; emphasizing instead the importance of culture and ideology.

Revolutions of 1848: a wave of revolutions in Europe that occurred in the spring of 1848 and were primarily democratic in nature.

Rhetoric: an art that aims to improve the capability of writers or speakers to persuade an audience.

Rise of the West: the processes through which Western European countries achieved global political and economic supremacy.

Russian Revolution of 1917: a revolution that led to the collapse of the Romanov dynasty, and the foundation of a communist republic.

Saur Revolution: a 1978 revolution in which the communist People's Democratic Party of Afghanistan overthrew then president Mohammed Daoud Khan.

Social theorists: scholars who develop frameworks for interpreting social phenomena.

Sociology/sociologist: the study of the nature, constitution, and history of human societies; a sociologist conducts this study.

Soil exhaustion: the process through which soil loses its fertility and becomes barren, usually via over-farming.

Soviet Union: a state on the Eurasian continent that existed between 1922 and 1991. It was dissolved in 1991, following revolutions that overthrew Soviet rule in many Central and Eastern European countries.

Structural determinism: the belief that social and economic structures are the sole and determining force of historical change, human behavior, culture, and ideas.

Structural weaknesses: weaknesses in a state's ability to govern that are expressed in military defeats, loss of control by the state over competing elites, and popular disorder.

Third World: refers to countries with colonial pasts that are widely seen to depend on "first world" countries such as the United States, France, Britain, and Germany.

Tokugawa Shogunate: a military dynasty that ruled Japan from 1600 until the political reforms of 1868, known as the Meiji Restoration.

Tradition-repudiating ideologies: philosophical outlooks that challenge orthodoxies and social hierarchies.

Transcultural/transhistorical: used to describe characteristics applicable throughout and across human history, and not merely a single society or historical period.

United States Agency for International Development: the principal American federal agency responsible for providing civilian foreign aid.

Yellow Revolution: a series of popular demonstrations in the Philippines between 1983 and 1986 that culminated in the ousting of President Ferdinand Marcos.

World Bank: an international monetary institution that provides loans to developing countries.

World War II: a global war fought between 1939 and 1945 between the extremely right-wing forces of Nazi Germany and its allies in Japan and Italy, and the Axis forces, led by Britain, the Soviet Union, and the United States.

PEOPLE MENTIONED IN THE TEXT

Keith Michael Baker (b. 1938) is a British historian at Stanford University. He has written several foundational works on the intellectual origins of the French Revolution.

Stephen Broadberry (b. 1956) is a British economic historian, working at the London School of Economics. He specializes in the comparative history of economic growth.

Joseph M. Bryant is a Canadian historical sociologist at the University of Toronto. His research has focused primarily on religion in classical antiquity.

Alfred Cobban (1901–68) was a British historian, best known for attacking the Marxist interpretation of the French Revolution in his *Social Interpretation of the French Revolution*.

Richard Cobb (1917–96) was a British historian of revolutionary France. He contested the Marxist interpretation of the French Revolution through detailed case studies of social life in eighteenth-century provincial France.

Randall Collins (b. 1941) is an American sociologist who is currently a professor at the University of Pennsylvania. He has written a number of theoretical works on the nature of social conflict.

Paul R. Ehrlich (b. 1932) is an American biologist at Stanford University. He is best known for his predictions about the cataclysmic effects of population growth and resource exhaustion.

Shmuel N. Eisenstadt (1923–2010) was a Polish-born Israeli sociologist who held a number of academic posts worldwide, predominantly at the Hebrew University in Jerusalem. He taught Goldstone while a guest professor at Harvard.

François Furet (1927–97) was a French historian, noted for challenging Marxist interpretations of the French Revolution in his seminal *Interpreting the French Revolution*.

Andre Gunder Frank (1929–2005) was a German American economic historian. He specialized in the comparative history of global economic development.

Bishnupriya Gupta is a British historian at the University of Warwick. She specializes in the history of industrial development in India.

Eric Hobsbawm (1917–2012) was a British Marxist historian. His best-known work is a trilogy on the "long nineteenth century."

George Homans (1910–89) was an American sociologist and a founder of behavioral sociology.

Lynn Hunt (b. 1945) is an American historian at the University of California Los Angeles. She has written several works emphasizing the role of culture in the origins of the French Revolution.

Eric Jones (b. 1936) is an English historian best known for his book *The European Miracle: Environments, Economies and Geopolitics in the History of Europe and Asia*, which traces the rise of Western Europe to economic and cultural transformations that began during the Renaissance.

Peter Laslett (1915–2001) was an English historian. He wrote influential books on the demographic history of seventeenth-century England, and co-founded the Cambridge Group for the History of Population and Social Structure in 1964 with Edward Anthony Wrigley.

Thomas Malthus (1766–1834) is widely considered to be the founder of modern demography. His *Essay on the Principle of Population* (1798) described the relationship between long-term population trends and various natural and social factors.

Ferdinand Marcos (1917–89) was the president of the Philippines from 1965 to 1986.

Karl Marx (1818–83) was a German philosopher. His ideas were foundational to the discipline of sociology and the development of the communist movement in the nineteenth and twentieth centuries. He argued that historical change was the outcome of class struggle between capitalists and the working class.

Barrington Moore Jr. (1913–2005) was an American political sociologist. He wrote influential comparative histories that traced the evolution of political systems in Europe, the United States, and Asia.

Joseph Needham (1900–95) was a British historian who wrote extensively about Chinese science. He argued in his multi-volume *Science and Civilization in China* that Taoism and Confucianism ultimately prevented the scientific breakthroughs that occurred in Europe from the seventeenth century onward.

Geoffrey Parker (b. 1943) is a British historian. He is best known for his work on the military revolution of the sixteenth century.

Kenneth Pomeranz (b. 1958) is an American historian whose work has focused on the economic history of early modern China.

Eric Selbin is a political scientist at Southwestern University. His primary area of research focuses on revolutions.

Theda Skocpol (b. 1947) is an American sociologist and political scientist at Harvard University. She is a pioneer of the comparative approach to the study of historical revolutions and a mentor to Jack Goldstone.

Lawrence Stone (1919–99) was an English historian noted for his work on the English Civil War.

Charles Tilly (1929–2008) was an American sociologist. He published numerous works on the social, political, and technological development of Europe from the Middle Ages to the present.

Alexis de Tocqueville (1805–59) was a French political thinker. He is best known for his works on the French Revolution and the democratic institutions of nineteenth-century America.

Immanuel Wallerstein (b. 1930) is an American sociologist. He is best known for his view that the origin of the modern world system can be traced to the emergence of capitalism in northwestern Europe in the sixteenth century.

Jeffrey Wasserstrom (b. 1961) is an American historian at the University of California, Irvine. His work focuses on social movements in twentieth-century China.

Max Weber (1864–1920) was a German sociologist. He defined the state as an entity that holds a monopoly on the legitimate use of force and violence.

Sam White is an American historian at Ohio State University. He specializes in the global history of the environment.

Roy Bin Wong (b. 1949) is a Chinese American economic historian at the University of California Los Angeles. He is best known for his contribution to the Great Divergence debate.

Edward Anthony Wrigley (b. 1931) is a historical demographer. He cofounded the Cambridge Group for the History of Population and Social Structure in 1964 with Peter Laslett.

WORKS CITED

WORKS CITED

Broadberry, Stephen, and Bishnupriya Gupta. "The Early Modern Great Divergence: Wages, Prices and Economic Development in Europe and Asia, 1500-1800." *Economic History Review* 59, no. 1 (2006): 2–31.

Bryant, Joseph M. "A New Sociology for a New History? Further Critical Thoughts on the Eurasian Similarity and Great Divergence Theses." *Canadian Journal of Sociology* 22 (Spring 2008): 149–67.

———. "The West and the Rest Revisited: Debating Capitalist Origins, European Colonialism and the Advent of Modernity." *Canadian Journal of Sociology* 31 (2006): 403–44.

Collins, Randall. "Maturation of the State-Centered Theory of Revolution and Ideology." *Sociological Theory* 11 (March 1993): 117–28.

Dunning, Chester. "Does Jack Goldstone's Model of Early Modern State Crises Apply to Russia?" *Comparative Studies in Society and History* 39 (July 1997): 572–92.

Goldstone, Jack A. "Analyzing Revolutions and Rebellions: A Reply to Critics." In *Debating Revolutions*, edited by Nikki R. Keddie, 178–99. New York: New York University Press, 1995.

———. "Capitalist Origins, the Advent of Modernity, and Coherent Explanation: A Reply to Joseph M. Bryant." *Canadian Journal of Sociology* 33 (2008): 119–33.

———. "Demography and Security." In *Security and Development in Global Politics*, edited by Joanna Spear and Paul D. Williams, 271–90. Washington, DC: Georgetown University Press, 2012.

———. "Gender, Work, and Culture: Why the Industrial Revolution Came Early to England and Late to China." *Sociological Perspectives* 39, no. 1 (Spring 1996): 1–21.

———. "Historical and Comparative Theory." In *Encyclopedia of Social Theory I*, edited by George Ritzer, 134–9. Thousand Oaks, CA: SAGE Publications, 2005.

———. "The New Population Bomb: Four Population Megatrends That Will Shape The Global Future." *Foreign Affairs* 89, no. 1 (February 2010): 31–43.

———. "Population and Progress in the Middle Ages." *Population and Development Review* 27 (2001): 585–96.

———. Population Growth and Revolutionary Crises. In *Theorizing Revolutions*. Edited by John Foran. London: Routledge, 1997.

_____. Population Movements and Conflict. In *The International Studues Encyclopedia Vol.9*. Edited by Robert A Denemark. Chichester, West Sussex: Wiley-Blackwell, 2010.

———. "The Problem of the 'Early Modern' World." *Journal of the Economic and Social History of the Orient* 41, no. 3 (1998): 249–84.

———. "Rethinking Revolutions: Integrating Origins, Processes, and Outcomes." *Comparative Studies of South Asia, Africa, and the Middle East* 29 (2009): 8–32.

———. *Revolution and Rebellion in the Early Modern World*. Berkeley, CA: University of California Press, 1991.

———. "The Rise of the West – or Not? A Revision to Socio-Economic History." *Sociological Theory* 18, no. 2 (2000): 175–94.

———. "The 'Stress' Revolution." *New York Review of Books*. April 22, 1993.

———. "Theories of Revolution: The Third Generation." *World Politics* 32, no. 3 (1980): 425–53.

———. "Using Quantitative Models to Forecast Instability." *US Institute of Peace, Special Report 204* (March 2008).

———. *Why Europe? The Rise of the West in World History, 1500-1800*. New York: McGraw-Hill, 2008.

Goldstone, Jack, Daniel C. Esty, Ted Robert Gurr, Barbara Harff, Pamela T. Surko, Alan N. Unger, and Robert Chen. "The State Failure Project: Early Warning Research for US Foreign Policy Planning." In *Preventive Measures: Building Risk Assessments and Crisis Early Warning Systems*, edited by John Davies and Ted R. Gurr, 27–38. Boulder: Rowman and Littlefield, 1998.

Gunder Frank, Andre. *ReOrient: Global Economy in the Asian Age*. Berkeley, CA: University of California Press, 1998.

Hobsbawm, Eric. *The Age of Revolution: Europe 1789–1848*. UK: Abacus, US: Vintage, 1962.

Parker, Geoffrey. "Crisis and Catastrophe: The Global Crisis of the Seventeenth Century Reconsidered." *American Historical Review* 113 (October 2008): 1053–79.

Pomeranz, Kenneth. *Great Divergence: China, Europe and the Making of the Modern World Economy*. Princeton: Princeton University Press, 2000.

Selbin, Eric. "Revolution in the Real World: Bringing Agency Back In." In *Theorizing Revolutions*, edited by John Foran. London; New York: Routledge, 1997.

Skocpol, Theda. *States and Social Revolutions: A Comparative Analysis of France, Russia and China*. Cambridge: Cambridge University Press, 1979.

Stone, Lawrence. ."The Revolution Over the Revolution." *New York Review of Books*. June 11, 1992.

———. "The 'Stress' Revolution: Lawrence Stone replies." *New York Review of Books*. April 22, 1993.

Tilly, Charles. "The Bourgeois Gentilhommes of Revolutionary Theory." In *Debating Revolutions*, edited by Nikki Keddie, 136–45. New York: New York University Press, 1995.

Vries, Peer. "The California School and Beyond: How to Study the Great Divergence." History Compass 8, no. 7 (2010): 730–51.

Wasserstrom, Jeffrey. "Bringing Culture Back In and Other Caveats: A Critique of Jack Goldstone's Recent Essays on Revolution." In *Debating Revolutions*, edited by Nikki R. Keddie, 155–78. New York: New York University Press, 1995.

White, Sam. *The Climate of Rebellion in the Early Modern Ottoman Empire*. Cambridge: Cambridge University Press, 2011.

_____. "The Little Ice Age Crisis of the Ottoman Empire: A Conjuncture in Middle East Environmental History." In *Water on Sand: Environmental Histories of the Middle East and North Africa*, edited by Alan Mikhail. Oxford; New York: Oxford University Press, 2012.

Wong, Roy Bin. *China Transformed: Historical Change and the Limits of European Experience*. Ithaca: Cornell University Press, 1997.

THE MACAT LIBRARY
BY DISCIPLINE

The Macat Library By Discipline

AFRICANA STUDIES

Chinua Achebe's *An Image of Africa: Racism in Conrad's Heart of Darkness*
W. E. B. Du Bois's *The Souls of Black Folk*
Zora Neale Huston's *Characteristics of Negro Expression*
Martin Luther King Jr's *Why We Can't Wait*
Toni Morrison's *Playing in the Dark: Whiteness in the American Literary Imagination*

ANTHROPOLOGY

Arjun Appadurai's *Modernity at Large: Cultural Dimensions of Globalisation*
Philippe Ariès's *Centuries of Childhood*
Franz Boas's *Race, Language and Culture*
Kim Chan & Renée Mauborgne's *Blue Ocean Strategy*
Jared Diamond's *Guns, Germs & Steel: the Fate of Human Societies*
Jared Diamond's *Collapse: How Societies Choose to Fail or Survive*
E. E. Evans-Pritchard's *Witchcraft, Oracles and Magic Among the Azande*
James Ferguson's *The Anti-Politics Machine*
Clifford Geertz's *The Interpretation of Cultures*
David Graeber's *Debt: the First 5000 Years*
Karen Ho's *Liquidated: An Ethnography of Wall Street*
Geert Hofstede's *Culture's Consequences: Comparing Values, Behaviors, Institutes and Organizations across Nations*
Claude Lévi-Strauss's *Structural Anthropology*
Jay Macleod's *Ain't No Makin' It: Aspirations and Attainment in a Low-Income Neighborhood*
Saba Mahmood's *The Politics of Piety: The Islamic Revival and the Feminist Subjec*t
Marcel Mauss's *The Gift*

BUSINESS

Jean Lave & Etienne Wenger's *Situated Learning*
Theodore Levitt's *Marketing Myopia*
Burton G. Malkiel's *A Random Walk Down Wall Street*
Douglas McGregor's *The Human Side of Enterprise*
Michael Porter's *Competitive Strategy: Creating and Sustaining Superior Performance*
John Kotter's *Leading Change*
C. K. Prahalad & Gary Hamel's *The Core Competence of the Corporation*

CRIMINOLOGY

Michelle Alexander's *The New Jim Crow: Mass Incarceration in the Age of Colorblindness*
Michael R. Gottfredson & Travis Hirschi's *A General Theory of Crime*
Richard Herrnstein & Charles A. Murray's *The Bell Curve: Intelligence and Class Structure in American Life*
Elizabeth Loftus's *Eyewitness Testimony*
Jay Macleod's *Ain't No Makin' It: Aspirations and Attainment in a Low-Income Neighborhood*
Philip Zimbardo's *The Lucifer Effect*

ECONOMICS

Janet Abu-Lughod's *Before European Hegemony*
Ha-Joon Chang's *Kicking Away the Ladder*
David Brion Davis's *The Problem of Slavery in the Age of Revolution*
Milton Friedman's *The Role of Monetary Policy*
Milton Friedman's *Capitalism and Freedom*
David Graeber's *Debt: the First 5000 Years*
Friedrich Hayek's *The Road to Serfdom*
Karen Ho's *Liquidated: An Ethnography of Wall Street*

John Maynard Keynes's *The General Theory of Employment, Interest and Money*
Charles P. Kindleberger's *Manias, Panics and Crashes*
Robert Lucas's *Why Doesn't Capital Flow from Rich to Poor Countries?*
Burton G. Malkiel's *A Random Walk Down Wall Street*
Thomas Robert Malthus's *An Essay on the Principle of Population*
Karl Marx's *Capital*
Thomas Piketty's *Capital in the Twenty-First Century*
Amartya Sen's *Development as Freedom*
Adam Smith's *The Wealth of Nations*
Nassim Nicholas Taleb's *The Black Swan: The Impact of the Highly Improbable*
Amos Tversky's & Daniel Kahneman's *Judgment under Uncertainty: Heuristics and Biases*
Mahbub Ul Haq's *Reflections on Human Development*
Max Weber's *The Protestant Ethic and the Spirit of Capitalism*

FEMINISM AND GENDER STUDIES

Judith Butler's *Gender Trouble*
Simone De Beauvoir's *The Second Sex*
Michel Foucault's *History of Sexuality*
Betty Friedan's *The Feminine Mystique*
Saba Mahmood's *The Politics of Piety: The Islamic Revival and the Feminist Subject*
Joan Wallach Scott's *Gender and the Politics of History*
Mary Wollstonecraft's *A Vindication of the Rights of Woman*
Virginia Woolf's *A Room of One's Own*

GEOGRAPHY

The Brundtland Report's *Our Common Future*
Rachel Carson's *Silent Spring*
Charles Darwin's *On the Origin of Species*
James Ferguson's *The Anti-Politics Machine*
Jane Jacobs's *The Death and Life of Great American Cities*
James Lovelock's *Gaia: A New Look at Life on Earth*
Amartya Sen's *Development as Freedom*
Mathis Wackernagel & William Rees's *Our Ecological Footprint*

HISTORY

Janet Abu-Lughod's *Before European Hegemony*
Benedict Anderson's *Imagined Communities*
Bernard Bailyn's *The Ideological Origins of the American Revolution*
Hanna Batatu's *The Old Social Classes And The Revolutionary Movements Of Iraq*
Christopher Browning's *Ordinary Men: Reserve Police Batallion 101 and the Final Solution in Poland*
Edmund Burke's *Reflections on the Revolution in France*
William Cronon's *Nature's Metropolis: Chicago And The Great West*
Alfred W. Crosby's *The Columbian Exchange*
Hamid Dabashi's *Iran: A People Interrupted*
David Brion Davis's *The Problem of Slavery in the Age of Revolution*
Nathalie Zemon Davis's *The Return of Martin Guerre*
Jared Diamond's *Guns, Germs & Steel: the Fate of Human Societies*
Frank Dikotter's *Mao's Great Famine*
John W Dower's *War Without Mercy: Race And Power In The Pacific War*
W. E. B. Du Bois's *The Souls of Black Folk*
Richard J. Evans's *In Defence of History*
Lucien Febvre's *The Problem of Unbelief in the 16th Century*
Sheila Fitzpatrick's *Everyday Stalinism*

The Macat Library By Discipline

Eric Foner's *Reconstruction: America's Unfinished Revolution, 1863-1877*
Michel Foucault's *Discipline and Punish*
Michel Foucault's *History of Sexuality*
Francis Fukuyama's *The End of History and the Last Man*
John Lewis Gaddis's *We Now Know: Rethinking Cold War History*
Ernest Gellner's *Nations and Nationalism*
Eugene Genovese's *Roll, Jordan, Roll: The World the Slaves Made*
Carlo Ginzburg's *The Night Battles*
Daniel Goldhagen's *Hitler's Willing Executioners*
Jack Goldstone's *Revolution and Rebellion in the Early Modern World*
Antonio Gramsci's *The Prison Notebooks*
Alexander Hamilton, John Jay & James Madison's *The Federalist Papers*
Christopher Hill's *The World Turned Upside Down*
Carole Hillenbrand's *The Crusades: Islamic Perspectives*
Thomas Hobbes's *Leviathan*
Eric Hobsbawm's *The Age Of Revolution*
John A. Hobson's *Imperialism: A Study*
Albert Hourani's *History of the Arab Peoples*
Samuel P. Huntington's *The Clash of Civilizations and the Remaking of World Order*
C. L. R. James's *The Black Jacobins*
Tony Judt's *Postwar: A History of Europe Since 1945*
Ernst Kantorowicz's *The King's Two Bodies: A Study in Medieval Political Theology*
Paul Kennedy's *The Rise and Fall of the Great Powers*
Ian Kershaw's *The "Hitler Myth": Image and Reality in the Third Reich*
John Maynard Keynes's *The General Theory of Employment, Interest and Money*
Charles P. Kindleberger's *Manias, Panics and Crashes*
Martin Luther King Jr's *Why We Can't Wait*
Henry Kissinger's *World Order: Reflections on the Character of Nations and the Course of History*
Thomas Kuhn's *The Structure of Scientific Revolutions*
Georges Lefebvre's *The Coming of the French Revolution*
John Locke's *Two Treatises of Government*
Niccolò Machiavelli's *The Prince*
Thomas Robert Malthus's *An Essay on the Principle of Population*
Mahmood Mamdani's *Citizen and Subject: Contemporary Africa And The Legacy Of Late Colonialism*
Karl Marx's *Capital*
Stanley Milgram's *Obedience to Authority*
John Stuart Mill's *On Liberty*
Thomas Paine's *Common Sense*
Thomas Paine's *Rights of Man*
Geoffrey Parker's *Global Crisis: War, Climate Change and Catastrophe in the Seventeenth Century*
Jonathan Riley-Smith's *The First Crusade and the Idea of Crusading*
Jean-Jacques Rousseau's *The Social Contract*
Joan Wallach Scott's *Gender and the Politics of History*
Theda Skocpol's *States and Social Revolutions*
Adam Smith's *The Wealth of Nations*
Timothy Snyder's *Bloodlands: Europe Between Hitler and Stalin*
Sun Tzu's *The Art of War*
Keith Thomas's *Religion and the Decline of Magic*
Thucydides's *The History of the Peloponnesian War*
Frederick Jackson Turner's *The Significance of the Frontier in American History*
Odd Arne Westad's *The Global Cold War: Third World Interventions And The Making Of Our Times*

LITERATURE

Chinua Achebe's *An Image of Africa: Racism in Conrad's Heart of Darkness*
Roland Barthes's *Mythologies*
Homi K. Bhabha's *The Location of Culture*
Judith Butler's *Gender Trouble*
Simone De Beauvoir's *The Second Sex*
Ferdinand De Saussure's *Course in General Linguistics*
T. S. Eliot's *The Sacred Wood: Essays on Poetry and Criticism*
Zora Neale Huston's *Characteristics of Negro Expression*
Toni Morrison's *Playing in the Dark: Whiteness in the American Literary Imagination*
Edward Said's *Orientalism*
Gayatri Chakravorty Spivak's *Can the Subaltern Speak?*
Mary Wollstonecraft's *A Vindication of the Rights of Women*
Virginia Woolf's *A Room of One's Own*

PHILOSOPHY

Elizabeth Anscombe's *Modern Moral Philosophy*
Hannah Arendt's *The Human Condition*
Aristotle's *Metaphysics*
Aristotle's *Nicomachean Ethics*
Edmund Gettier's *Is Justified True Belief Knowledge?*
Georg Wilhelm Friedrich Hegel's *Phenomenology of Spirit*
David Hume's *Dialogues Concerning Natural Religion*
David Hume's *The Enquiry for Human Understanding*
Immanuel Kant's *Religion within the Boundaries of Mere Reason*
Immanuel Kant's *Critique of Pure Reason*
Søren Kierkegaard's *The Sickness Unto Death*
Søren Kierkegaard's *Fear and Trembling*
C. S. Lewis's *The Abolition of Man*
Alasdair MacIntyre's *After Virtue*
Marcus Aurelius's *Meditations*
Friedrich Nietzsche's *On the Genealogy of Morality*
Friedrich Nietzsche's *Beyond Good and Evil*
Plato's *Republic*
Plato's *Symposium*
Jean-Jacques Rousseau's *The Social Contract*
Gilbert Ryle's *The Concept of Mind*
Baruch Spinoza's *Ethics*
Sun Tzu's *The Art of War*
Ludwig Wittgenstein's *Philosophical Investigations*

POLITICS

Benedict Anderson's *Imagined Communities*
Aristotle's *Politics*
Bernard Bailyn's *The Ideological Origins of the American Revolution*
Edmund Burke's *Reflections on the Revolution in France*
John C. Calhoun's *A Disquisition on Government*
Ha-Joon Chang's *Kicking Away the Ladder*
Hamid Dabashi's *Iran: A People Interrupted*
Hamid Dabashi's *Theology of Discontent: The Ideological Foundation of the Islamic Revolution in Iran*
Robert Dahl's *Democracy and its Critics*
Robert Dahl's *Who Governs?*
David Brion Davis's *The Problem of Slavery in the Age of Revolution*

The Macat Library By Discipline

Alexis De Tocqueville's *Democracy in America*
James Ferguson's *The Anti-Politics Machine*
Frank Dikotter's *Mao's Great Famine*
Sheila Fitzpatrick's *Everyday Stalinism*
Eric Foner's *Reconstruction: America's Unfinished Revolution, 1863-1877*
Milton Friedman's *Capitalism and Freedom*
Francis Fukuyama's *The End of History and the Last Man*
John Lewis Gaddis's *We Now Know: Rethinking Cold War History*
Ernest Gellner's *Nations and Nationalism*
David Graeber's *Debt: the First 5000 Years*
Antonio Gramsci's *The Prison Notebooks*
Alexander Hamilton, John Jay & James Madison's *The Federalist Papers*
Friedrich Hayek's *The Road to Serfdom*
Christopher Hill's *The World Turned Upside Down*
Thomas Hobbes's *Leviathan*
John A. Hobson's *Imperialism: A Study*
Samuel P. Huntington's *The Clash of Civilizations and the Remaking of World Order*
Tony Judt's *Postwar: A History of Europe Since 1945*
David C. Kang's *China Rising: Peace, Power and Order in East Asia*
Paul Kennedy's *The Rise and Fall of Great Powers*
Robert Keohane's *After Hegemony*
Martin Luther King Jr.'s *Why We Can't Wait*
Henry Kissinger's *World Order: Reflections on the Character of Nations and the Course of History*
John Locke's *Two Treatises of Government*
Niccolò Machiavelli's *The Prince*
Thomas Robert Malthus's *An Essay on the Principle of Population*
Mahmood Mamdani's *Citizen and Subject: Contemporary Africa And The Legacy Of Late Colonialism*
Karl Marx's *Capital*
John Stuart Mill's *On Liberty*
John Stuart Mill's *Utilitarianism*
Hans Morgenthau's *Politics Among Nations*
Thomas Paine's *Common Sense*
Thomas Paine's *Rights of Man*
Thomas Piketty's *Capital in the Twenty-First Century*
Robert D. Putman's *Bowling Alone*
John Rawls's *Theory of Justice*
Jean-Jacques Rousseau's *The Social Contract*
Theda Skocpol's *States and Social Revolutions*
Adam Smith's *The Wealth of Nations*
Sun Tzu's *The Art of War*
Henry David Thoreau's *Civil Disobedience*
Thucydides's *The History of the Peloponnesian War*
Kenneth Waltz's *Theory of International Politics*
Max Weber's *Politics as a Vocation*
Odd Arne Westad's *The Global Cold War: Third World Interventions And The Making Of Our Times*

POSTCOLONIAL STUDIES

Roland Barthes's *Mythologies*
Frantz Fanon's *Black Skin, White Masks*
Homi K. Bhabha's *The Location of Culture*
Gustavo Gutiérrez's *A Theology of Liberation*
Edward Said's *Orientalism*
Gayatri Chakravorty Spivak's *Can the Subaltern Speak?*

PSYCHOLOGY

Gordon Allport's *The Nature of Prejudice*
Alan Baddeley & Graham Hitch's *Aggression: A Social Learning Analysis*
Albert Bandura's *Aggression: A Social Learning Analysis*
Leon Festinger's *A Theory of Cognitive Dissonance*
Sigmund Freud's *The Interpretation of Dreams*
Betty Friedan's *The Feminine Mystique*
Michael R. Gottfredson & Travis Hirschi's *A General Theory of Crime*
Eric Hoffer's *The True Believer: Thoughts on the Nature of Mass Movements*
William James's *Principles of Psychology*
Elizabeth Loftus's *Eyewitness Testimony*
A. H. Maslow's *A Theory of Human Motivation*
Stanley Milgram's *Obedience to Authority*
Steven Pinker's *The Better Angels of Our Nature*
Oliver Sacks's *The Man Who Mistook His Wife For a Hat*
Richard Thaler & Cass Sunstein's *Nudge: Improving Decisions About Health, Wealth and Happiness*
Amos Tversky's *Judgment under Uncertainty: Heuristics and Biases*
Philip Zimbardo's *The Lucifer Effect*

SCIENCE

Rachel Carson's *Silent Spring*
William Cronon's *Nature's Metropolis: Chicago And The Great West*
Alfred W. Crosby's *The Columbian Exchange*
Charles Darwin's *On the Origin of Species*
Richard Dawkin's *The Selfish Gene*
Thomas Kuhn's *The Structure of Scientific Revolutions*
Geoffrey Parker's *Global Crisis: War, Climate Change and Catastrophe in the Seventeenth Century*
Mathis Wackernagel & William Rees's *Our Ecological Footprint*

SOCIOLOGY

Michelle Alexander's *The New Jim Crow: Mass Incarceration in the Age of Colorblindness*
Gordon Allport's *The Nature of Prejudice*
Albert Bandura's *Aggression: A Social Learning Analysis*
Hanna Batatu's *The Old Social Classes And The Revolutionary Movements Of Iraq*
Ha-Joon Chang's *Kicking Away the Ladder*
W. E. B. Du Bois's *The Souls of Black Folk*
Émile Durkheim's *On Suicide*
Frantz Fanon's *Black Skin, White Masks*
Frantz Fanon's *The Wretched of the Earth*
Eric Foner's *Reconstruction: America's Unfinished Revolution, 1863-1877*
Eugene Genovese's *Roll, Jordan, Roll: The World the Slaves Made*
Jack Goldstone's *Revolution and Rebellion in the Early Modern World*
Antonio Gramsci's *The Prison Notebooks*
Richard Herrnstein & Charles A Murray's *The Bell Curve: Intelligence and Class Structure in American Life*
Eric Hoffer's *The True Believer: Thoughts on the Nature of Mass Movements*
Jane Jacobs's *The Death and Life of Great American Cities*
Robert Lucas's *Why Doesn't Capital Flow from Rich to Poor Countries?*
Jay Macleod's *Ain't No Makin' It: Aspirations and Attainment in a Low Income Neighborhood*
Elaine May's *Homeward Bound: American Families in the Cold War Era*
Douglas McGregor's *The Human Side of Enterprise*
C. Wright Mills's *The Sociological Imagination*

The Macat Library By Discipline

Thomas Piketty's *Capital in the Twenty-First Century*
Robert D. Putman's *Bowling Alone*
David Riesman's *The Lonely Crowd: A Study of the Changing American Character*
Edward Said's *Orientalism*
Joan Wallach Scott's *Gender and the Politics of History*
Theda Skocpol's *States and Social Revolutions*
Max Weber's *The Protestant Ethic and the Spirit of Capitalism*

THEOLOGY

Augustine's *Confessions*
Benedict's *Rule of St Benedict*
Gustavo Gutiérrez's *A Theology of Liberation*
Carole Hillenbrand's *The Crusades: Islamic Perspectives*
David Hume's *Dialogues Concerning Natural Religion*
Immanuel Kant's *Religion within the Boundaries of Mere Reason*
Ernst Kantorowicz's *The King's Two Bodies: A Study in Medieval Political Theology*
Søren Kierkegaard's *The Sickness Unto Death*
C. S. Lewis's *The Abolition of Man*
Saba Mahmood's *The Politics of Piety: The Islamic Revival and the Feminist Subjec*t
Baruch Spinoza's *Ethics*
Keith Thomas's *Religion and the Decline of Magic*

COMING SOON

Chris Argyris's *The Individual and the Organisation*
Seyla Benhabib's *The Rights of Others*
Walter Benjamin's *The Work Of Art in the Age of Mechanical Reproduction*
John Berger's *Ways of Seeing*
Pierre Bourdieu's *Outline of a Theory of Practice*
Mary Douglas's *Purity and Danger*
Roland Dworkin's *Taking Rights Seriously*
James G. March's *Exploration and Exploitation in Organisational Learning*
Ikujiro Nonaka's *A Dynamic Theory of Organizational Knowledge Creation*
Griselda Pollock's *Vision and Difference*
Amartya Sen's *Inequality Re-Examined*
Susan Sontag's *On Photography*
Yasser Tabbaa's *The Transformation of Islamic Art*
Ludwig von Mises's *Theory of Money and Credit*